Ministering to Families

A Positive Plan of Action

A·C·U PRESS

Royce Money

Library of Congress Catalog Card Number 86-72162

ISBN- 0-915547-92-9

Dedication

This book is affectionately dedicated
to the Highland Church of Christ
in Abilene, Texas—my spiritual family
who is teaching me daily the meaning of love
and acceptance in the family of God.
To Him be the glory!

Table of Contents

Page

Foreword

A church is as strong as the families and single people who compose it. Church leaders spring from families. Today's families, even in strong churches, are waging a fierce battle to preserve the integrity of family life in a secular world. So this book provides a real solution to churches who are serious about their ministry to families.

It has been my personal privilege to know Royce, Pam and their girls for a number of years. He served as the first Family Life Minister of the South National Church of Christ. He did his work so well that Abilene Christian University hired him to train other Family Life Ministers for congregational work.

The approach in this book is solidly Biblical and intensely practical. Church leaders frequently ask questions like, "How do we minister to families? How can we best assess the needs of families? What are the practical approaches of family ministry?" This book certainly helps answer these questions.

All of us have our family life as a common denominator. How we are doing is often measured by our family life. So in a world where families are literally falling apart, this book serves to respond to a crucial need. Whether you are a church leader, a family member, or a general reader interested in knowing more about families, you will find this book to be most useful.

Prentice A. Meador, Jr.
Minister, South National Church of Christ
Springfield, Missouri

"Today the church is on the edge of many great decisions. But certainly one of the most significant is this: Are we willing to do what must be done for the church to help the family face the future? Or will we abandon the nuclear family to face essentially alone these forces it was not designed to overcome without the support of the body?"

Larry Richards, *"How the Church Can Help the Family Face the Future"* (Plenary Session, St. Louis Continental Congress on the Family, 1975), p. 15.

Chapter 1
Ministering to Families–An Introduction

What Ministering To Families Is About

Is your family important to you? Very few people would answer no to that question. If you are like most Christians, you recognize that in many ways the family is the foundation for our society and our church life. In its proper perspective, the family is a great blessing from God. Through the family, God provides for our basic needs, including our need for love, affection, and a sense of belonging. Through the family, God helps us grow and mature, preparing us for lifelong fruitful roles in society. Through the family, God blesses others, just as He promised Abraham to bless all people on earth through his offspring (Gen. 12:3).

But the family is in trouble. The breakdown of traditional family patterns has been hastened by declining moral standards, the cultural rise of individualism, and other forces of change and "progress" in society. Is it any wonder that current figures for family breakups, domestic violence, and crime are at all-time highs?

The fact that you are reading this book shows that you care about the family. You want to reach out and help the hurting people in your church and community. You want others to experience all the blessings God gives through healthy Christian families. But where do you begin? Which direction do you head? How should you proceed?

These and other questions must be answered before we Christians can effectively reach out to families. That's what this book is about. Perhaps this is the first book on family ministry you have ever picked up to read. You have a deep concern for what is happening to families and you want to do something about it as a caring Christian. Perhaps you have had a greater degree of involvement and interest in a ministry to families in a church setting that has directed your attention to this present work. Whatever the background or motive, *Ministering to Families* will hopefully offer you practical help and insight in your involvement with families in your church and community.

Above all, *Ministering to Families* is for those people who are *committed to doing something* about disintegrating family life among Christians and in the community at large. The material is designed to challenge your thinking about family issues facing all of us and to stimulate you to appropriate action.

Many churches already have a family life committee; others have not yet organized such a group. What is most important at this point is the commitment to help enrich the family experiences of others in your church and community. A strong commitment to the family will help unite you and others in your church in reaching out to families.

Ministering to Families will guide you as you consider people's needs, types of programs that could benefit families, and where to begin. *Ministering to Families* is not a textbook on family ministry; in other words, it does not treat exhaustively theoretical issues dealing with the family. Nor does it tell you what family-oriented programs your church needs. Rather, *Ministering to Families* addresses important questions that help you plan what is needed and what to do. It helps the leaders and members of your church discuss a range of issues and options, then take practical steps to address the needs of families in your church and community. It is a book that is designed to be used—written in and discussed. It is designed with *your involvement* in mind.

The *process* you and others will go through as you grow and develop in your leadership capabilities in this area of concern is as important as the content you'll learn. In fact, you may not agree with all the concepts presented—that's fine. The information is meant to challenge your thinking.

The book is designed so that it can be read in its entirety by an individual who desires greater insights into Christian family ministry. But the maximum effectiveness is best reached when the material is shared—perhaps in a small group, or in a committee, or in a Bible class that emphasizes ministry to others. The *heart* of the process is contained in the various group activities contained at the end of each chapter. It is in the small group setting, where Christians can work together to discuss, evaluate, and then apply the principles in the book to your own church context, that the material really comes alive.

So you are a key to the effective use of this study program. Take this opportunity to commit yourself to the prayer and preparation necessary for each group session so that God can use you to help your church reach out to families in a meaningful way.

How To Use This Book

As I have just indicated, *Ministering to Families* can be used in a variety of ways—from introducing an individual to the world of family ministry to giving step-by-step guidelines to family life committees who want to begin an effective family ministry in a church.

The rest of this introductory chapter deals with the latter category—those who will be using the group activities material at the end of each chapter. If you are in the former category—the interested individual—you may want to skip over the rest of this chapter and begin with Chapter 2. No hard feelings on my part.

Now to those who will be using the material in a group setting. The primary purpose in writing this material is to facilitate Christian people who want to see their congregation more involved in an effective ministry to families. The interest in families may come from an education committee, youth committee, family life committee, or simply from several families who come together out of a common concern about Christian family life and values. Or the interest may come from church leaders who are concerned about the families in their charge and don't know what to do about the problems they see there.

The Family Life Committee

The group of people responsible for coordinating your church's ministry to families is commonly called a family life committee. In some churches, this committee or one similar to it will already be in existence. But for those churches who have not organized in that way and who are just beginning a family emphasis, here are some practical guidelines the leaders should observe as a committee is being formed:

1 Make sure the committee reflects the makeup of your church. You need to have a good mix in age and gender and also a representative blend according to marital status. Those who are divorced, never married, and widowed have distinct viewpoints and needs that should be represented on the committee. You may wish to add additional factors that would insure a good cross-section of the congregation on your committee.

2 Look for people with special gifts in areas that are critical to an effective family ministry. For example, a person familiar with local media management or one with public relations experience would be valuable in promoting the ministry programs. Others may have organizational skills that could be effectively used.

3 Get people to serve who aren't already overburdened in other ministries. There's some truth to the old saying, "If you want something done, get a busy person to do it," but this piece of advice has limitations. Churches are full of extremely talented people whose gifts are not being used by the church to the glory of God. Look for these people and get them involved.

4 Rather than asking one spouse in a family to serve, you might consider involving both husband and wife. It provides something of a team approach that allows both to spend their energies on a common service. Those who are not married need to be a part of a committee, as well. A blend of married couples and singles is good.

5 Because of the diversity of procedures among churches, it is difficult to say what degree of involvement the paid staff or volunteers should have on the committee. Certainly they should be consulted and kept informed, but whether or not they are on the committee is a matter for each church to decide.

Who is on your family life committee and how they are chosen are extremely important factors in determining the shape that a ministry to families will take. Perhaps several words of caution are in order:

1 In order for a committee to be efficient, it cannot be too large. But the smaller a committee is, the more difficult it is to be truly representative. Committees which, in effect, appoint themselves need to be somewhat self-critical. It may be difficult to answer the question, "Who isn't on the committee—and should be?" But failing to ask that question makes it more likely that the family ministry—when adopted by the church—will tend to serve the interests and needs of the committee members and others like them better than other types of people and families.

2 The active participation of women on a family life committee is important. If a committee is largely comprised of men, with only a few token women, the church's family ministry will probably have two major difficulties. First, the service programs planned by the committee may not be as relevant to the needs of female family members. Second, the committee may have difficulty getting women of the church actively involved in implementing the church's program and in feeling "ownership" for it.

3 Getting families involved in ministry to other families is one of the vital concerns presented in the ninth chapter. Giving responsibility and power to family members for planning and decision-making is a key step in increasing relevance and ownership in a family ministry. If a family life committee cannot actually put certain people on the committee, it can find ways to involve them in responsible planning. Forming advisory committees or special task forces are possibilities. Many youth groups have sponsor or parent councils which serve this purpose.

4 Family ministry is an on-going process. Over time, people change. They perceive new needs, change their interests, and grow in their ability to handle responsibility. The committee structure should be flexible enough to permit people to get involved when they are ready— not several years down the road when someone's serving time expires. Perhaps the committee does not need a fixed number of members but can incorporate people as they wish. Whatever the case, nonmembers of the committee should be permitted to attend some of its regular meetings.

Scheduling

Ministering to Families can be used in ten consecutive weeks or it can be used in sub-units. For example, your church might want to have an organized meeting using Group Activity session 1, then study sessions 2 through 4, take a break, then work through sessions 5 through 8, and then complete sessions 9 and 10. The content would easily lend itself to this sequence. Other churches may study two sessions a week and complete the program in five weeks. The book also lends itself well to a midweek evening format for a Bible class or a family ministry study group. Some churches may want to use the program at a series of weekend leadership retreats, either at the church or away from it. For example, they could use the first session before the retreat, then they could study sessions 2, 3, and 4 on a Friday evening and Saturday morning. On a second Friday evening and Saturday morning they could complete sessions 5-8. Then they could use sessions 9 and 10 on the third Saturday morning. The chapters should be read and the application activities completed before the retreats. About ten hours will be needed to complete all the group sessions.

The materials should be adapted to your situation. But a word of caution is necessary. Because of the interrelationship of the sessions, it's better not to spread the program out over a long period of time (such as a year), because the program would lose its continuity. In addition, if a church tries to use the program too quickly (for example, all day on a Saturday), the participants will find it difficult to absorb the content.

Leader's Guides

Ministering to Families does not have a separate leader's guide because each of the group members can be the leader of one or more of the sessions. Every group member will be given the opportunity to volunteer to serve as a session leader. All necessary instructions for session leaders are included in each session.

Book Format

Each chapter in the book (after this introductory chapter) contains "Application Activities" for you to read and complete. These activities are designed so that you can interact with the material as you read and be able to apply it in a practical way to your own setting. In some cases, the activities will provide the basis for the discussion in your group meeting. Because each student will be writing in his or her own book, it is essential for every participant to have his or her own book.

At the end of each chapter will be a "Group Activity" section. It will consist of a suggested agenda from which the leader may choose whatever items time and group interest will permit. The leader can be the same person each time, but I would suggest that the privilege be passed around among the individuals who feel comfortable doing it. All information the group leader will need is contained in each Group Activity session.

Leadership and Administrative Functions

Your group will need someone to care for the following functions so this program can operate smoothly. (One person could easily care for more than one function.)

1 *Leading each session.* See subsequent sections of this chapter for a description of the session leader and his responsibilities.

2 *Tabulating responses to the congregational questionnaire and/or neighborhood interviews introduced* *in Chapter 4.* If either of these instruments is used, someone needs to tabulate the responses and make a copy for each group member by session 9. To tabulate the responses, add the total number of responses to each item and determine percentages based on the number of people who answer each question. Responses to open-end questions should be categorized when possible and significant verbatim quotes recorded.

3 *Recording and collecting group ideas.* In several of the sessions group members are asked to make a special application of the materials to your local church situation. In some cases, the ideas that are generated—about a particular problem or possible program—may be of value to your church's family ministry committee or other leaders at a later time. Someone needs to be responsible for collecting these ideas (which will usually be written on newsprint), and occasionally typing them.

Terminology Used in Ministering to Families

This study may be used by people from various backgrounds. Because people often use the *same* words with *different* meanings, you need to understand how specific words are used in this book for a better understanding of the materials and their use.

1 *Family.* A family is a group of two or more persons related by blood or marriage. Most commonly, *family* refers to parents and their children, but its meaning as used in *Ministering to Families* should not be restricted to members of the so-called "nuclear family". Grandparents, adopted children, stepchildren, and other members of households may also be included, depending on the context and the readers' backgrounds.

2 *Family ministry.* Church programs or actions which seek to serve the interests of families make up a church's family ministry.

3 *Church.* This designation refers to the church of Jesus Christ. It may not always be clear to the reader whether the worldwide church or the local congregation is intended. This is unavoidable. Confusion will usually be clarified by the context in which the term appears.

4 *Church Member.* Church member refers to any true believer who regularly worships and participates in the work of a local church and who claims membership there.

5 *Group Session Leader.* Group leader or session leader means a group participant who, by mutual agreement, is responsible for providing direction to a group meeting and for making decisions on behalf of the group about how that meeting's agenda will be followed. The group leader is *not* a person who teaches or talks the most. The group leader is *not* responsible to see that learning takes place: that is the responsibility of all group members. I recommend that there be a different leader for each session. At the close of each meeting, opportunity will be given for a group leader to volunteer for the next session. (See the next section for information about the function of a group leader.)

6 *Leader. Ministering to Families* is designed to be used by a group of leaders and interested members in a local church who are responsible for coordinating a ministry to families. By leader, I mean anyone who has decision-making responsibility for the family life ministry, not necessarily a person who holds an "office" or official position in the church. Church elders, deacons, and ministers are, of course, all leaders in their respective areas of service. But I encourage users of these materials to invite anyone who has a special gift in areas that are critical to an effective family ministry to participate as a member of the family life committee. There may be people in the church who have no decision-making responsibilities, yet they are recognized as gifted and committed individuals. Perhaps some have held leadership positions in the church in past years. Such people can be included in these leadership training sessions.

7 *Participant.* Participant refers to every member of the group using these materials. Usually some decision-making body in a church will decide who will be asked to participate. The people who accept and commit themselves to studying the materials and meeting with the group or class are participants.

Tips For Members and Leaders

In group meetings, each of you will perform leadership responsibilities as participants. You will share the responsibility of learning by actively participating in the group discussions in order to reach your goals.

Though all group members are responsible for leadership functions, someone will volunteer to serve the group as the discussion leader for each session. This person will help coordinate the interaction among the group participants. *The leader will not necessarily know the most about the topic and will not try to lead the group to accept his own conclusions.* Whenever possible, the leader will let the group work together without assistance.

The roles and responsibilities of all group participants and the session leader are listed below.

Group Participants

The role of all group participants:

1 Be prepared to discuss, based on your reading, previous experiences, and activities.

2 Help to decide which discussion questions the group will consider.

3 Share ideas and experiences relating to discussion topics.

4 Encourage others to give opinions and information.

5 Help others to communicate clearly.

6 Help keep the discussion on track.

7 Listen actively.

8 Build on others' ideas.

9 Help the group work out conflicts and problems.

10 Pray for each other.

11 Volunteer to lead a session.

12 Encourage others by regular, prompt attendance at sessions.

The Group Process

Because the group which will be studying this program of ministry in your church will probably be small, you will all be able to participate freely and naturally in the discussions. You'll find that the group discussions will actually become more like group conversations as you begin talking to one another without waiting for a question to be asked or to be called on by a leader. As each of you shares your thoughts and opinions about each session's study, you'll gain a deeper and broader understanding of the Scriptures and their application to both your life as an individual and the life of your church.

This group interaction will also help create open and honest friendships between all members of the group, which in turn will make the group discussions more natural and meaningful for you and your church. This in-depth involvement will also make it easier for each of you to share the things you're learning with other people in the church, whether they are your friends, your Bible study group, your Bible class, or your church committee. When that sharing begins to happen, you'll begin to sense a growing enthusiasm and expectancy for what God is going to accomplish through your lives together as His church.

Session Leaders

The role of the session leader:

1 Assist the group in selecting the discussion questions to be considered.

2 Initiate discussion.

3 Encourage freedom of expression and participation by all group members.

4 Encourage teamwork.

5 Help participants communicate with each other.

6 Help the discussion move along according to the subject and purpose intended.

7 Try to prevent one or two persons from dominating the discussion.

8 Keep the group aware of the time schedule for the agenda.

Leading Discussions

Here are a few guidelines to help make the most of the discussion time when you are the group's session leader:

1 *Allow time for the group to think.* Don't be afraid of short periods of silence. Avoid jumping in with your own answers or opinions just to fill in the time. Try not to make a contribution to the discussion that someone else in the group can make.

2 *Respect every individual's comments.* Everyone needs to be free to say what he *does* think, not what he *should* think. Make it clear that everyone's ideas and thoughts are welcome.

3 If needed, you may want to *ask follow-up questions* after an individual's comments to help him amplify his thoughts and to move from an abstract idea to a practical application.

4 *Stay close to Scripture.* The Bible is the authority behind this study and it must be the touchstone for all your discussions in order for your conclusions to be meaningful to your church's ministry.

5 *Challenge any superficial or trite answers that are given.* Do not be satisfied with merely quoting a Bible verse or using cliches or phrases that are familiar but hold little meaning. Ask what is meant. Ask for illustrations.

6 If some members seem hesitant to participate, you may want to *ask them direct questions*—especially those involving opinions or personal experience.

7 If some members are too talkative, *you may want to begin addressing questions to others by name.* After the meeting ask the talkative people to help encourage everyone in the group to participate in the discussion in future meetings.

Implementing Your Family Ministry

Laying a Foundation

In any church ministry, it is important that leaders understand what they are doing, why they are doing it, and why it is important. Chapters 2 through 5 lay this foundation for a family ministry in your church. Chapter 2 gives an introduction to family ministry concepts and terms. For example, the distinction between prevention—keeping specific family problems from occurring—and enrichment—promoting the overall health of families—is made. Also, the role of the church and the roles of family members themselves in carrying out a ministry to families is discussed. In your church's family ministry, you will want to make sure that church-run programs for families do not undermine the ability of parents to care for the health of their own children. Rather, church and family need to work together as partners if both are to benefit from the planned programs.

Family ministry must be relevant to the real needs of families. Chapter 3 highlights a number of current social trends that threaten the well-being of families. By discussing contemporary family life and problems, you and other church members will be able to plan family-oriented activities and programs that are "on target" with the needs of families in your congregation and community.

Determining what needs the families in your congregation and community have is a key step. Different methods for assessing these needs—including a congregational questionnaire and community interview—are discussed in Chapter 4.

No church family ministry can be successful unless it is based on principles drawn from God's Word. What does the Bible say about the family? How important is the family to God? Why should the church reach out to families? What should be the church's purpose in carrying out a ministry to families? The biblical foundation for family ministry is presented in Chapter 5.

Planning Family Ministry

Good church programs do not just happen. They begin with careful thought, planning, and prayer. No one can tell you and other leaders in your church exactly what to do. Only leaders who understand and have worked in your local context can do that. But you can learn from the difficulties others have encountered in beginning a family ministry. Many practical issues must be faced, though your response to each issue will be unique. Chapters 6 and 7 help lay the foundation for a ministry to families. The ideas offered in these two sessions will help you consider many facets of family ministry; they will challenge you to broaden your thinking about family ministry and how to implement one in your congregation.

In family ministry it is important to maintain the positive strengths of family life. Rather than only reaching out to those families in crises, family ministry needs to demonstrate patterns of healthy family ministry. Chapter 8 discusses seven characteristics or traits of healthy, Christian families.

In all decisions, leaders in your church need to identify particular problems, focus on actual needs, and set goals for your family ministry. Chapters 6 through 8 will help leaders recognize problems in your congregation and set priorities for your family ministry.

Getting Started

Chapters 9 and 10 will help you plan the first steps in beginning a family ministry. Introducing any new program in a church is difficult—many things can go wrong. People resist change, even if it is a change they perceive as being good! Chapter 9 helps you answer some vital questions before introducing a new approach to family ministry to your church.

Chapter 10 suggests steps you can take to get started in planning for family ministry. It will help you understand the results of the congregational questionnaire and community questionnaire introduced in Chapter 4. You will begin to make plans for family ministry. Finally, your family life committee will need to present its plan for a family ministry to the congregation in order to gain their long-term support of and participation in the ministry.

Our families are important to us, as the families of our friends and neighbors are important to them and to God. He wants strong families that are committed to Him and to one another, who will honor Him in all of life. The church's family ministry is a crucial part of God's plan to extend His rule—in this generation and the next. May He guide you as you seek to serve Him by serving the family!

Group Activities

Preparation for Group Meeting

Instructions for All Participants

Check off the following items as you prepare for the group meeting:

- ☐ Read the introductory chapter.
- ☐ Look over the agenda for session 1.
- ☐ Make a note of questions or comments you have about what you have read for this session (discuss them under agenda item 4).
- ☐ Pray that God will use these materials to help your church reach out to families.

Leader's Instructions:

Preparation

- ☐ *Read the tips for session leaders (chapter 1).*
- ☐ *Read the meeting agenda thoroughly. All leader's instructions are in italics and set off by horizontal rules.*
- ☐ *Give each group member a book at least one week before the first session, if possible. Ask them to read the first chapter and read through the agenda for the group activity.*

Materials Needed

- ☐ *Newsprint and markers or chalkboard and chalk.*

Group Meeting Agenda

1. Opening

- ☐ *If this study session is part of the regular meeting of a committee or class, check with the person in charge on the procedure for introducing this part of the meeting. Otherwise begin the session with prayer.*

2. Large group activity (10 minutes)

Have group members share how their family upbringing may have helped prepare them for leadership or involvement roles in the church.

- ☐ *Record the ideas shared by group members on a chalkboard or newsprint.*
- ☐ *The purpose of this activity is to foster appreciation for the family as a gift from God to individuals and to His church. Do not be afraid of brief silences—this lets people reflect on their own experiences and thank God for their families.*

3. Group discussion (15 minutes)

1. What questions do you have about the format and procedure for using this study program?
2. Who do you think should be added to your family life committee or class to make it representative of the types of families in your church?

3 How do you feel about *change*—change in traditional family patterns and ways of life, change in the way the church ministers to families? Do you welcome such changes, or do you avoid them when possible? How do you think the members of your congregation feel about each of these types of change?

4 Discuss the following statement: "God's people have become desensitized to all the modern evils that are tearing apart the family. The world is so much a part of the church, that Christians just don't care anymore. They are apathetic, they have lost the vision of what God makes possible in the family, and they have little or no compassion for people who have broken family lives. It's so common today that it is just accepted." To what extent does this reflect your attitude toward family problems? Is it true of the congregation's feelings?

- ☐ *Allow everyone's views and comments to be heard.*
- ☐ *Use this time to come up with a plan for organizing the future group meetings.*
- ☐ *Ask for a volunteer to lead the next meeting.*

4. Close in prayer.

NOTES

“At its heart family-life ministry is related to the nature of the church, not merely to its work. Family-life ministry is not a mere appendage to the church’s organization. Like missions, it must be integrated into the church’s life.”

Charles Sell, *Family Ministry,* p. 74

Chapter 2
What Is a Ministry To Families?

A Challenge to Church Leaders

Church leaders deal with a variety of family experiences and circumstances within their fellowships. These varied backgrounds of members can be an asset rather than a liability to church life. As Christian leaders and involved members, we have a choice in the *way* we minister to families in our congregations. We can sit back and let things happen as they will and step in only during a crisis. This choice is family ministry by default. Or we can build an approach to family ministry that is positive, enriching, and preventive—one which also provides assistance for those in crises.

Most churches fall somewhere between these two extremes in family ministry. However, all churches can improve their ministry to families. That's what serving families is about. Welcome to the exciting world of ministry to families!

What Is A Family?

To understand what we mean by the term *family ministry,* we must first define *family.*

The concept of family can be divided into two broad categories. The first is referred to as the *biological family*—those we are related to because of common blood relationships or through the marriage of one of our blood relatives. Biological families include the nuclear or immediate family and the greater or extended family. The extended family consists of grandparents, cousins, aunts, uncles, and in-laws.

The second category is the *functional family.* A "family" may not be biologically related, but they can function as a family. For example, adopted children have functional families that often are more dear to them than their biological parents (even if the natural parents are known). Foster children also fit into this category. On another level, each of us at some time has unofficially "adopted" someone or an entire family who function like a biological family. This practice is particularly true when we are separated from our natural kin. Thus, it is possible for a person to belong to several different "families" at various points in life.

The conclusion is that the word "family" has various meanings to people in our churches and in society—family can mean biological, functional, or both. To other people the term "family" may mean very little. Church family ministries need to be especially sensitive to the isolated people.

In trying to answer the complicated question of "What is a family?" several observations might be helpful.

1 Everyone is profoundly influenced by the family context in which he or she is raised. The influence may be unrecognized, but it is nevertheless powerful and present throughout life. However, any negative influences can be altered and overcome.

2 Families span several generations. First Timothy 5:3-8 shows the Christian that family obligations extend beyond one's immediate kin to the larger family. That larger family also includes in-laws.

3 By definition, one person cannot constitute a family. Some type of interpersonal relationships must exist, either biological or functional. Today, there is an increasing number of family types. The church can serve people in these "families" as long as they do not pursue an unbiblical lifestyle.

4 Single people—whether divorced, never married, or widowed—need a functional family relationship. The church is uniquely equipped for this purpose. Perhaps the greatest ministry the church has to singles is to provide for them a functional, spiritual family-like atmosphere. In such a loving and accepting context, Christian brothers and sisters can literally become more meaningful to the single person than his or her own biological family.

5 Families are greatly influenced by the culture in which they find themselves. Cultural differences may appear in opinions on: the view of the extended family, sex roles, division of labor, family expectations, customs, and what is socially acceptable. The church must be sensitive to cultural and ethnic differences in the role and function of the family.

6 From a Christian perspective, it is important for families to affirm the biblical values and principles which may be part of their culture. Cultural patterns which are unchristian have to be changed. This task can be difficult to do, but the biblical teachings on human relationships are eternal and transcend all cultures.

Churches are made up of a variety of family types with varying needs. The task of church leaders is to recognize these needs and blend them with the healing, helping power of the Gospel.

Application Activities

1. Identify all the living people you consider part of your family. Write the names of your family members and their relationship to you on the following diagram. Are all blood relatives? Are there any others who you aren't sure belong to your family? What are their relationships to you? (Add other circles and lines as needed.)

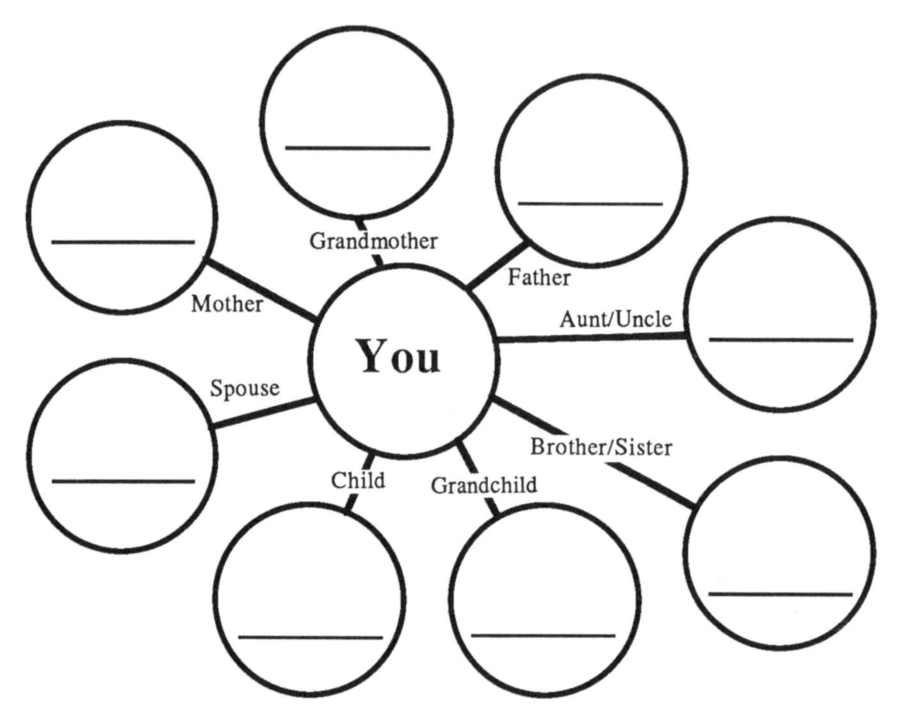

2. What feelings come to mind when you hear the word "family"? What types of experiences led you to have these feelings?

Looking At Family Ministry

Now that we have an initial understanding of what *family* means, we can consider some characteristics of *family ministry.* Family ministry is the major focus of Ministering to Families, but throughout this unit we will be looking at the many facets of family: family roles and responsibilities, family life cycles and transition points, pressures on the family, needs and problems of the Christian family. My hope is that you learn more about the changing patterns of American families so your church can enhance its total *ministry* to families.

What is *family ministry?* In one sense, this entire unit is a definition of family ministry. But it might be helpful to focus briefly on what family ministry is *not:*

1 Family ministry is not simply a building or a facility. Though buildings might be used for family ministry purposes, our concern for families emphasizes programs of ministry and involvement, rather than facilities.

2 Family ministry is not merely a catalog of church or community programs. These activities are only a part of our efforts.

3 Family ministry is not another appendage to a continually growing church program. Like evangelism and missions, family ministry must be integrated into every aspect of church life.

4 Family ministry is not a passing fad. It lies at the core of what it means to be a community of believers.

5 Family ministry is not just for nuclear families—mom, dad and children. It is relevant to everyone's needs.

6 Family ministry is not just for church families. It provides an excellent means for believers to reach out into the community by ministering to the needs of other families.

7 Family ministry is not merely a counseling service. Some families may need specialized attention, but most families can be helped through positive emphasis on enrichment and growth.

8 Family ministry doesn't have to be expensive. Great expenditures of money are not needed for a church to minister to its families. Later, I will be talking about how any church can begin a ministry to families that keeps within the church's talents and financial means.

In short, family ministry is a total approach to families—an outlook. The essence of family ministry is an attitude toward the family that must be integrated into every aspect of church life. Family ministry involves a style of servant leadership that is dedicated to making the church a community of vibrant families. It emphasizes home-centered nurture and nurture found through the church. Concern for individual families within the greater family of God is central to the church's identity and mission. *The church is more like a family than anything else.*

Application Activities

1. How would you characterize your church's approach to families? List several areas of strengths and needed improvement.

Strengths

1 ______________________________

2 ______________________________

3 ______________________________

Needed improvement

1

2

3

2. After reviewing the descriptions of what a family ministry is not, write what you think a church family ought to be.

Prevention and Enrichment

Recently a Christian educator remarked, "It sure does make more sense to build a fence around the edge of a cliff than to put an ambulance at the bottom." He made this point after observing a family ministry program that was preventive in nature. The only way we can slow down or stop family disintegration is by strengthening our families so that major problems won't arise. We can teach families skills that will help them prevent major problems from disrupting their lives. An ounce of prevention—applied while families are teachable and before turmoil erupts—is worth a ton of cure, and a lot easier to do!

The heart of preventive "fence-building" is teaching effective problem-solving techniques and conflict-resolution skills. This emphasis will help stop harmful family patterns from developing. Serious marital and family problems have small beginnings. The traditional response of the church to family troubles has been "reactive"—waiting for problems to surface, then (when it's really too late) trying to do something about them. The church's family ministry needs to be more "pro-active" in its approach: recognizing the forces at work before family conflicts become serious, and working to promote healthy family relationships and patterns all the time.

Effective family ministry will reflect positive teaching which focuses on problems and conflicts while they are still manageable. A positive approach builds on what the Bible says about members of the body of Christ getting along with one another. It emphasizes the day-to-day skills needed to keep family members in harmony with each other and with God.

Marriage is one family relationship that can be greatly enriched through preventive forms of ministry. Various types of marriage enrichment programs and experiences serve as catalysts for improved marriage relationships. Every marriage, no matter what its condition, can be improved. A family ministry emphasis can have significant results and provide opportunity for much growth in this vital area.

Church and Family Partnership

Ministering to Families will emphasize the need for the church and the individual family to work as partners. Each can make a positive contribution that the other cannot. In many cases, the home is overly dependent on the church, especially for the spiritual training of children. Deuteronomy 6:6–9 reminds us that the spiritual direction for the family must primarily come from within the home and cannot be delegated to others:

> *These commandments that I give you today are to be upon your hearts. Impress them on your children. Talk about them when you sit at home and when you walk along the road, when you lie down and when you get up. Tie them as symbols on your hands and bind them on your fore-*

heads. Write them on the door frames of your houses and on your gates.

The purpose of this study is to provide guidance toward a *balanced* approach to family nurture. That means not placing too much emphasis on the institutional church's role, nor placing all the burden on individual families. The church as an organization can enhance the family life of its members, but it cannot do everything. Achieving a balanced approach means that a family ministry must help parents assume greater responsibility for the spiritual nurture of their families, as the entire church family supports and encourages individual families.

One of the beautiful things about Christian families is that we can help each other. Dual parent families can help single parent families. Older, more experienced couples can help younger ones. Singles who have no family members of their own nearby can be "adopted" by other families and add a meaningful dimension to those families. The same is true of widows and orphans. We need each other, and a dynamic family ministry helps facilitate "one-anothering."

Application Activities

1. "Translate" the principles contained in Deuteronomy 6:6–9 into modern terms. What would Moses say to us today as parents? What would he have parents do in caring for the moral well-being of their children?

2. Earlier in the chapter, the marriage relationship was used as an example of an area where a family ministry can have a significant impact both in a preventive ministry and in times of crisis. The same is true of other family relationships. Choose one of the following key relationships (or suggest another of your own).

Examples:

Parent-child relationship
Adult child-parent relationship
Grandparent-child-grandchild relationship

1. List some of the typical problems that can arise in that relationship.

2. In what ways can the church help prevent those problems?

3. In what ways can a family ministry help family members cope with problems in that relationship if they become serious?

Group Activities

Preparation for Group Meeting

Instructions for All Participants

Check off the following items as you prepare for the group meeting:

- ☐ *Read the chapter and complete the application activities.*
- ☐ *Look over the agenda for session 2.*
- ☐ *Make a note of any questions or comments you have about what you have read for this session (discuss them under agenda item 3).*
- ☐ *Write down your thoughts or reactions to the discussion questions suggested under agenda item 3.*

- ☐ *Pray about concerns you've become aware of through your preparation for this session.*

Leader's Instructions:

Preparation

- ☐ *Read the tips for session leaders (chapter 1).*
- ☐ *Read the chapter and the group activity agenda for session 2.*
- ☐ *Complete the exercises given in chapter 2.*
- ☐ Read all the leader's instructions (indicated in italics) before the meeting begins.

Materials Needed

- ☐ *Newsprint, markers, masking tape.*

Group Meeting Agenda

1. Opening

- ☐ *If this study session is part of the regular meeting of a committee or class, check with the person in charge on the procedure for introducing this part of the meeting. Otherwise begin this session with prayer.*

2. Large group activity (10 minutes)

Group members share with the entire group how they described what a family ministry should be. (Refer to the application activity 4.)

- ☐ *List key ideas on newsprint or a chalkboard as they are shared.*

3. Large group discussion (20–25 minutes)

- ☐ *Ask the group which topics listed below they would like to discuss.*
- ☐ *In addition, at this time individuals may bring up questions or comments they had about the chapter for consideration by the entire group.*

Discussion topics:

1. Which of the ideas or characteristics of a family ministry listed under agenda item 2 do you feel are most important for your church's family ministry? Why?
2. What do you think are some prevailing opinions in your church about what a family ministry is? What factors or experiences in the history of your church or community may have influenced the way people think about family ministry?
3. "People who have problems with anger in the home, divorce, or child abuse don't need a 'family ministry'—they need the Gospel." Discuss.

4. Dreaming about your family ministry (in small groups) (10 minutes)

What do you hope your family ministry could accomplish in five years' time? What dreams do group members have for an effective ministry to families in your church and community? (For the moment, forget about the practicality, costs, or other details of achieving these goals.)

- ☐ *Divide the group into separate, small groups of 4–5 people per group.*
- ☐ *Each small group should have a recorder and a reporter.*

5. Share ideas with large group (5–10 minutes)

- ☐ *Ask the reporter for each group to share its ideas with the large group.*
- ☐ *As the ideas are being shared, summarize each one briefly on the chalkboard or newsprint.*

Group participants may make comments on ideas from other small groups.

- ☐ *When all ideas have been shared, the group may wish to identify three or four that are central to the purpose of a family ministry in your church. You may wish to make a permanent copy of these or all the goals for family ministry that were shared.*

6. Closing and prayer

- ☐ *Ask for a group member to volunteer to lead the next group meeting.*
- ☐ *Close in prayer.*

NOTES

“The past century has given birth to an institutional form of the church that lacks family dynamics. The church has become, first of all, a task-centered institution. . . . The result is, as in other task-oriented institutions, that relationships are viewed in the light of the job to be done. Each individual is noted and needed for his or her place in the corporate structure. The church's concern for maintaining relationships among Christians is often reduced to making certain people know their responsibilities (job description) and function with limited discord with others (work management).

Resulting relationships are superficial in this form of the church.”

Charles Sell, *Family Ministry,* p. 75

Chapter 3
The Need for a Ministry to Families

Comtemporary Family Life

We must never lose sight of the fact that many families in our nation are doing a pretty good job of living quality lives together. But they are in the minority. Many more families are experiencing struggle, conflict, frustration, bitterness, and disappointment. In this chapter we focus our attention on the suffering majority.

How would you characterize families today? Most experts agree that traditional family life is in trouble. Family breakups are occuring in record numbers, with no significant change in sight. The reasons for the current family problems are numerous. Here are some major factors contributing to family deterioration:

1 *Society is changing.* People are changing the way they work, play, where they live, and how they relate to others. Since World War II the *rate* of change in society has been growing faster and faster. Advanced technology has shifted the nation away from its industrial base. Today more people are spending their lives providing services for others (communications, banking, education, insurance, health) than in manufacturing or processing goods. In our computer-dominated world, the creation and processing of information has eclipsed the production of goods in our economy. The traditional ways of determining our identity (finding out who we are) and of associating with others (finding our place in society) have changed.

Family structures are also changing. The increasing number of single-parent families is staggering. Couples are waiting longer to marry (if they marry at all) and to have children (fewer per family unit than previous generations). Change of any kind is threatening; negative change is even more threatening.

2 *Families are isolated.* More than ever before, families are isolated from their kin—robbed of what in the past was a natural support system. Families are also isolated from neighboring families. Meaningful social contact with the community at large is also on the decline. The "family-turned-in-on-itself" has become a disturbing but accurate phrase describing modern American society.

3 *Families are mobile.* While from time to time, economic recesson may slow down moving, we are still a mobile society. Few things disturb family life more than a major move, especially if moves occur at frequent intervals. Security and stability of familiar surroundings and comfortable relationships are lost when a move occurs. Adjusting to a new environment can be difficult.

4 *Family members are insecure.* They are insecure about many things. For instance, roles within the family are less defined than they were a generation ago. This trend is not necessarily bad, but often makes us insecure about who we are and what we're supposed to be doing. Insecurities about marriage expectations, priorities, the economy, and the future are only a few of the things that leave today's families with unsettled feelings.

5 *People are lonely.* Today, perhaps more than at anytime in history, people are striving for intimacy and quality relationships. The quest for intimacy, often unrealistically viewed, may be a major cause of marriage breakups. This phenomenon, along with the other factors mentioned, leave many people lonely.

6 *Society is becoming more secular.* The shift away from a spiritual orientation to life is obvious among the general population. But the same is happening among Christian families. Christians are not immune from the shift toward secularism and materialism. The differences between Christian and non-Christian family lifestyles and priorities are becoming less obvious.

7 *Families are ill-equipped.* Modern living has produced its share of stress on the family. The ability to cope with these pressures and adapt to them is lagging behind. People seem to lack basic problem-solving skills, such as the ability to deal effectively with anger, conflict, frustration, and loneliness. Relationships—especially close ones—are incredibly complex in our modern world.

Application Activities

1. How are families in your community coping with the following problems? Put a check mark in the column you feel applies, and use the space between items to record any comments you have. (*See chart on page 40*)

2. Can you recall any facts or figures, newspaper articles, etc., that substantiate your impressions?

Issues	*Not a Problem*	*Here And There—Hear Of Isolated Cases*	*More Than Just A Few Cases—A Growing Concern*	*Lots Of People Looking For Answers*	*Out Of Hand*
Alcoholism					
Drug Abuse					
Spouse Abuse					
Divorce					
Suicide					
Teenage Pregnancy					
Child Abuse					
Homosexuality					

Implications for the Church

How do church leaders respond to the needs of a troubled world? How do they respond to family needs in their own communities, churches, or families? The answers are as varied as the needs. We must break down the needs into more manageable parts in order to get started. We might not be able to change the world the way we want. But we can change some people's worlds, as they touch our lives and those of the community of faith.

A place to start is to look at the general problems facing families in society at large, and then to decide what the implications are for today's church. Three possible conclusions follow; you will probably think of others.

1 *Christian families are affected by the same problems found in the rest of society.* Because we are *in* the world, we sometimes become a part of the world. Sin takes its toll on all our lives. We suffer from the same temptation God's people of old struggled with—how much and in what way they could be a part of a culture that did not know God. As a whole, the divorce record for Christians is not much better than society's. We wish we were immune from family and social problems, but we aren't. Church leaders need to know what Christian families are struggling with.

2 *The church's ministry to families needs to keep in mind the following social factors affecting modern families:*

Rapid pace of change
Family isolation
Increasing mobility
Insecurity over changing family roles
Loneliness
The secularization of society
Inability to cope with problems

Our approach to family ministry is one built around these and other needs. People will listen and respond to Christians offering help in coping with family stress and strain—if they see their needs being met. People may be more willing to listen to the Lord and His way during stressful times than at any other time in their lives! An effective ministry to families needs to be designed around the stress points of modern families—where the greatest need is.

3 *The church, through the power of the Gospel, has an answer for every social factor affecting today's families.* Isn't that Good News? God's church has the capacity to meet human needs at the deepest level in a way that nothing else can. Cultures come and go, but the needs of mankind remain the same—relationships with God and with one another. We, as Christians, have what people need and want. The *way* in which these answers are presented and these needs met makes a difference.

Do you believe God has the power to counter all the destructive forces that bombard the family today? Do you believe God can work through your church to meet the needs of families in your community? We, as Christians, can confidently accept the challenge God has given us to be involved in a ministry of healing relationships. How we do will demand the very best of our thoughts, prayers, and actions.

Application Activities

1. Repeat the exercise you did in which you looked at how families in your community are coping with various problems. This time, consider families in your church. How are they affected by these problems? (*See chart page 43*)

2. Review the chart and try to identify areas of greatest need. What are the areas you think should be given the greatest attention?

Issues	*Not a Problem*	*Here And There—Hear Of Isolated Cases*	*More Than Just A Few Cases—A Growing Concern*	*Lots Of People Looking For Answers*	*Out Of Hand*
Alcoholism					
Drug Abuse					
Spouse Abuse					
Divorce					
Suicide					
Teenage Pregnancy					
Child Abuse					
Homosexuality					

The Church's Response

What can we—the people of God—do to make a difference in this world? That's a challenging question. Our responses may be seen in light of this challenge God sets before us as leaders in the kingdom. He challenges us in at least three ways.

1 *To be salt, leaven, and light in a world that desperately needs our influence.* Church leaders have a choice to make. They can meet, vote, discuss, and debate with little action; or they can resolve to be in the world as a positive flavor, a positive force for good, and a source of much-needed light.

2 *To show the world the potential of Christian family life through teaching and example.* The amount of credibility a church leader has in his teaching is often tied to the example he sets. A church leader's family cannot be perfect. But a leader needs to show the way and convince others that a Christ-centered life has practical implications in the quality of one's own family life.

3 *To recapture and live out the family dynamic in our wider, church "family."* We will see in the next chapter that God uses the analogy of the family to describe His relationship to His people. We get our divine model for the church from the family—not from the corporate board room, political circles, or the business world. The church leader's challenge is to apply the same principles within the church that God gives us for experiencing a rich family life.

These challenges are not impossible. God does not dangle impossible dreams before His people. He always provides the resources with the challenge. Quality Christian family life is a part of the "full" life Christ desires for all His followers (John 10:10).

Application Activities

1. Stop for a few moments and pray that God will use you and your church in a powerful way in a healing ministry to families where you live.

Group Activities

Preparation for Group Meeting

Instructions for All Participants

Check off the following items as you prepare for the group meeting:

- ☐ *Read the chapter and complete the application activities.*
- ☐ *Look over the agenda for session 3.*
- ☐ *Make a note of any questions or comments you have about what you have read for this session (discuss them under agenda item 3).*
- ☐ *Write down your thoughts or reactions to the discussion questions suggested under agenda item 3.*
- ☐ *Pray about concerns you've become aware of through your preparation for this session.*

Leader's Instructions:

Preparation

- ☐ *Read the tips for session leaders (chapter 1).*
- ☐ *Read the chapter and the group activity agenda for session 3.*
- ☐ *Complete the exercises given in the chapter.*
- ☐ *Read all the leader's instructions (indicated in italics) before the meeting begins.*

Materials Needed

- ☐ *Newsprint, markers, masking tape.*

Group Meeting Agenda

1. Opening

- ☐ *If this study session is part of the regular meeting of a committee, or class, check with the person in charge on the procedure for introducing this part of the meeting. Otherwise begin this session with prayer.*

2. Small group activity (10–15 minutes)

This task involves the seven factors contributing to family deterioration described in the chapter:

- ☐ *rapid pace of change in society (1)*
- ☐ *family isolation (2)*
- ☐ *increasing family mobility (3)*
- ☐ *insecurity over changing family roles (4)*
- ☐ *loneliness (5)*
- ☐ *the secularization of society (6)*
- ☐ *inability to cope with problems (7)*

Task: discuss the above factors and decide which ones have the most affect on families in your church and community. In other words, which ones should be the focus of your church's family ministry in order to meet the needs of families in your community? After discussing the factors to make sure you understand what they mean, give each a priority in the following manner:

- ☐ *hold a "vote" for each of the seven factors.*
- ☐ *each person may cast three votes, and may distribute them*

anyway he wants among the seven factors (three votes for one factor, or one vote for three factors, etc.)

- ☐ *tally the group's votes for each of the seven factors.*
- ☐ *(Check the total number of votes: it should equal three times the number of people in your group.)*
- ☐ *Divide the group into separate, small groups of 4–5 people per group.*
- ☐ *Each group should appoint one person to tally the group's votes.*

3. Large group discussion (20–25 minutes)

- ☐ *Determine which of the following topics the group would like to discuss. To do this, collect the totals of the votes taken in each of the small groups. Add them together for each factor, and identify the two or three factors which received the highest number of votes. Question 1 through 7 correspond with each factor under agenda item 2, above. Questions 8 and 9 are optional questions, and they may also be discussed if group members wish and time permits.*

Discussion topics:

1 In what ways has your community changed in the last 20 years? What stresses or other problems have these changes brought for families? How is your community likely to change in the next 5 years? What can your church do to anticipate the future needs of families?

2 What are the causes that isolate families in your community from one another? (Consider such factors as geographic barriers, housing patterns, institutional groupings such as schools, employers, hospitals, county or township boundaries, social status based on wealth or education, ethnic distinctions, or time schedules.) Can your church do anything to break down or reduce the isolation of families in your community?

3 What special needs do families who just moved have? How can the church help them? How can the church help families that are in the process of moving away?

4 How can the church help the following family members: working mothers, unemployed husbands, latchkey children, the newly widowed or divorced, indecisive fathers, newlyweds?

5 Why are people lonely? Do you think the problem of loneliness is getting worse in your community? Why? Are there lonely people in your church? Can a church establish a separate program for lonely people, or is this a concern that has to cut across all church programs? How can church leaders generate concern for lonely people?

6 What influence(s) do you see the secular world having on your own family and other families in the church? (Consider the roles of public schools, the media, government.) How has this changed over the last 5 or 10 years? Where do you see the trend heading in the future? How can church leaders help parents combat this problem?

7 Are members of your church and community poorly equipped to deal with their family problems? Can or should your church provide training to assist people in gaining skills in interpersonal communication, effective listening, crisis counseling, etc.?

8 What obligation does the church have to influence the standards in the community which affect the quality of family life? Are there any particular areas where such action or influence is needed in your community?

9 To what extent do church leaders have the responsibility (and the right) to be involved in the lives of the families in their churches?

4. The importance of family ministry (in small groups) (5–10 minutes)

Small group 1 task: Discuss and list several possible answers to the following question: If your church had no emphasis on family ministry over the next five years, what difference would it make in your *church* at the end of that time?

Small group 2 task: Discuss and list several possible answers to the following question: If your church had no emphasis on family ministry over the next five years, what difference would it make in your *community* at the end of that time?

- ☐ *Divide the group into separate groups, with no more than five people per small group. If necessary, two or more groups may perform the same task.*
- ☐ *Each group should have a recorder and reporter for its ideas.*

5. Share ideas and insights with large group (5–10 minutes)

- ☐ *Ask the reporter from each group to share its answers to the question.*
- ☐ *After each group's ideas are given, you may want to allow a few minutes for comments and discussion.*

6. Closing and prayer

- ☐ *As group members reflect on the importance of family ministry and the consequences of not ministering to families, it may be appropriate to ask several people to pray for families in the church and community that God would guide church leaders in ministering to families.*
- ☐ *Ask for a group member to volunteer to lead the next group session.*

NOTES

“[The] approach of directing all energy toward family enrichment may ignore the impoverishment the family experiences when it is cut off from other people. Writers of evangelical literature on the home may be overlooking the individual's desperate need for community life as well as for a rich family life. . . .

We have begun to realize that the nuclear family is overloaded, in that it is expected to contribute more than it can to family health and well-being. The church's strategy should include finding means for the family to discover companionship and help outside itself.”

Charles Sell, *Family Ministry*, p. 48

Chapter 4
Assessing Family Needs

In chapter 3 we saw what families today face. It's obvious from contemporary trends in family patterns that the family needs help. But *what* help do families need? More specifically, what types of help do the families *in your church* need?

This chapter will help you begin to answer that question. You will be deciding what family needs are, how to go about assessing family needs in your community, how to use a family needs questionnaire with your congregation, and how to conduct family needs interviews in your community.

What Are Needs?

"I need a new baseball glove, Dad." "Grandma, you really need to eat better foods to stay healthy." "That salesclerk needs a lesson in politeness." "Two thousand refugees need temporary housing and winter clothes." "Millions need Christ."

Needs are hard to define. Most of us know what it is to struggle with decisions about whether we really *need* everything we *want.* "I want a new dress for the ladies' spring banquet, but I guess I don't really need a new one." On the other hand, sometimes we need things we don't really want. "I need to stop eating cake and candy, but I don't want to stop." How do we decide what we need?

It is even more difficult trying to determine the needs of *other people.* Sometimes they want things that aren't essential to their well-being. And sometimes they need things without wanting them or being aware of their own needs.

Trying to meet the needs of others is not easy. Sometimes we try to give something that nobody wants. Think of Christian missionaries who spend years working among people unresponsive to the Gospel. Sometimes our best intentions do more harm than good. Have you ever given money to a beggar, only to see him run to the nearest bar?

Family ministry is an attempt to help meet the needs of people, so it must be carefully planned to give appropriate help in meeting people's real needs. Church leaders deciding to help families should give careful thought to what families really need. The process of determining such needs is a key step in planning for family ministry. It is called *needs assessment.*

Family Needs

What do families need? And what are the particular needs of families in your church and community? These are two different-but-related questions. Material such as *Ministering to Families* can help answer the first question, but only you can answer the second question. By the time you finish chapter 4, you should have a clearer understanding of the answer to the first question. You should also understand how you and other leaders in your church can go about finding the answer to the second question.

Every time we make a claim about our needs or someone else's needs, we are actually stating a *belief* about what ought to be. We need food, clothing, and shelter because we believe life is important and we ought to preserve life. We need friends because we believe people should not be alone in the world. We need a saving relationship with Christ, because we believe that only through Him do we have forgiveness of sins and eternal life.

What do we believe about families? How do our beliefs about families affect the way we understand the needs of families? Here are five affirmations about the family that Christians can make:

1 Families need Christ to be the Lord of their homes, because we believe God created the family to bring glory to Himself through Christ (Ps. 145:4-7).

2 Family members need love for one another, because we believe only through love can the family survive the many trials of life (1 Cor. 13:7, Eph. 5:25).

3 Parents need to teach their children to love and obey God, because we believe God has given parents the responsibility to educate their children (Deut. 6:4-9).

4 Children need to honor their parents, because we believe God commands and rewards such respect (Eph. 6:1-2).

5 Family members need to feel secure in their homes, because we believe the threat of harm destroys love, trust, and harmony in the family (Col. 3:19, 21).

We can make many more affirmations about the family which will help us answer the question, "What do families need?" But what do we base our beliefs about family needs on? God's Word is the foundation on which every family ministry must be based. Without God's revelation of His will for His people, we would conclude all sorts of things based on our own opinions. We might believe, for example, that every family needs a maid, a butler, and two television sets. More will be said on the biblical basis for family ministry in chapter 5.

Application Activities

1. Which of the following do you think are needs which all families have? For each need that you agree with, state why you believe it is true. Is there any Scripture which supports your belief?

a. Husbands and wives *need* a commitment to each other for their marriage to last.

No.

Yes, I accept this, because I believe . . .

b. Couples *need* to have children in order to have a happy home.

No.

Yes, I accept this, because I believe . . .

c. Family members need to refrain from using substances which are harmful to their bodies.

No.

Yes, I accept this, because I believe . . .

d. Young children need to have at least one parent who does not work outside the home.

No.

Yes, I accept this, because I believe . . .

e. Families need to be involved in helping other people outside their home.

No.

Yes, I accept this, because I believe . . .

f. Parents need to help their children gain a biblical view of sex.

No.

Yes, I accept this, because I believe . . .

g. Adults need the freedom to raise their children without interference from the children's grandparents.

No.

Yes, I accept this, because I believe . . .

h. Family members need to learn to communicate with each other in constructive ways.

No.

Yes, I accept this, because I believe . . .

Assessing Family Needs

Perhaps you see that all families have needs. Of course, not all families are aware that they have these needs. Some Christian families may feel that they should not have needs or that they should not seek help for those needs. But from God's point of view, their needs are real nonetheless.

Not all needs are equally as important or pressing. Some families have more serious problems than other families. The process of determining what needs are most important to the people you are trying to help is a part of needs assessment.

If a family ministry committee is to plan effective programs, it must be in touch with the needs of the congregation and the community. Assessing family needs is an on-going process—people's needs and their perceptions of which needs are most important change. The aim of family needs assessment is to design and implement programs of service that are timely, relevant, and practical.

A standard approach to family needs assessment is for a family life committee to pass out a survey or questionnaire to the congregation. This procedure can be very helpful, but here are a number of pitfalls to avoid. One of the chief errors is assuming that once the committee has "data" on people's problems, they can "determine" people's needs. However, a number of other factors must be taken into account:

Before a family life committee assesses the needs of others, it must first *define its own beliefs* about what families ought to be like. For example, if committee members hold that every family should be made up of two parents living with their children, this belief will affect their view of others' needs. Single people will either "need" to be married or live at home with their parents. But this is not the way single people see their needs! Understanding the church's philosophy and biblical basis for family ministry is where a family life committee should begin.

Another important prelude to doing a needs assessment study is to *know the context* or environment in which the family ministry will operate. What trends in society put stress on families? What are the life concerns and commitments of people in the community? What services are already available to families and who provides them? And, most important, what are the real roots or causes of specific problems facing families?

Knowing who you are trying to help is essential in doing needs assessment. If a family ministry is to benefit Christian families in the church and non-Christian families in the community, a needs assessment must focus on both groups. In such a case, several methods of needs assessment should be used. A family needs questionnaire designed for congregational use would not be suitable for families in the community.

Family ministry planners need to understand that a needs assessment is *not a neutral tool* that leaves people unaffected. People's expectations are often raised after a congregational needs questionnaire is completed. Answering questions about their family needs may make people expect more from the church than it can deliver. If those expectations are not met, the result may be greater frustration or apathy. Consequently, a formal needs assessment (such as a printed questionnaire) is not always the most appropriate initial step in planning programs for families.

Needs assessment is not a panacea. The committee still needs to interpret the data collected and then act on it. *Deciding how specific types of information will be used* must be done *before* a needs assessment is carried out. Planners need to think about what they need to know and what results they intend for a needs assessment to have. For example, family ministry planners may think that they need to know all sorts of information about families in the community: communication patterns in the home, television viewing habits, divorce rates, etc. But unless the church has the capability to *use* such information in forming relevant family programs, there is little point in gathering the data.

Finally, the planning committee needs to consider what *methods* to use to better understand the needs of families in their church and community. Congregational surveys—when well thought out and carefully constructed for the local level—can be very helpful. But there are other equally valuable methods. Group dynamics methods (similar to some of the small group activities at the end of each chapter) can be helpful in identifying needs and ranking their relative importance. Interviews are helpful in understanding the complexity of the problems many families face. If trust can be established between interviewer and interviewee, one can gain insights to personal problems that could never be revealed by a questionnaire. Interviewing key leaders in the community, such as a child psychologist, school guidance counselor, or trained social workers can be especially valuable.

Family ministry planners can also gather data from secondary sources to find out more about the people they want to help. Data from the census bureau, local school districts, hospitals, national polls, religious surveys, or the local newspaper can be valuable.

Application Activities

1. Look through the last few issues of your local newspaper. Are there any articles that reveal current trends (such as unemployment or crime) or problems faced by particular families (minorities, elderly, widows)? Are there any articles that mention national trends affecting families (divorce rates, working patterns, legislation)?

What do these articles reveal about the needs of families in your community?

To what extent do families in your church have the same needs?

Bring the articles with you to your next group meeting. Continue to look for such articles in coming weeks.

2. Turn to appendix A, the Family Ministry Questionnaire, in the back of your book.

a. Read through the entire questionnaire. If you wish, answer the questions yourself based on your own family situation.

b. Go back and look at all the items on the questionnaire. Would each of these items be appropriate for your congregation? How could your family ministry committee *use* each type of information to plan family programs?

c. Suppose you and your family had just started attending your church. On your first Sunday, you were asked to fill out the questionnaire in appendix A. Assuming you knew little about the church, what might you expect to see in the way of family-oriented programs in the coming months?

d. Can you think of some items that are not included in the sample questionnaire, but would be valuable to your family life committee?

e. Can you think of some types of information that would be of value to your family life committee but which could not be obtained reliably from this or any other printed questionnaire?

Methods for Needs Assessment

What needs do families in your church and community have? How is your church able to help meet the more important needs of these families? These questions can only be answered by you, a group of leaders working at the local level to assess the needs of families. This portion of chapter 4 will consider how you might use two of the several possible methods for needs assessment: the congregational questionnaire and neighborhood interview.

First, why should you use either (or both) of these methods? After all, there are shortcuts to planning a family ministry. Leaders could act on the basis of their own understanding of others' needs to plan a family ministry. They could invite family life experts to give workshops on their favorite topics. Or they could look at what other churches in the community are doing and try to emulate their successes.

Each of these shortcuts, however, has two major problems. First, one group of people is trying to decide what another group of people needs without asking them directly. There is a danger of misunderstanding the problems and needs of families in our church and community. Any programs based on such misinformation risk being irrelevant or even harmful.

The second problem is that these shortcuts fail to involve people in planning to meet their own needs. An important goal for any family program is to encourage family members to take greater responsibility for the health and well-being of their families. Involving family members in the needs assessment is an important way to get families active in solving their own problems. In most types of church ministry, it is better to help people do something for themselves rather than merely providing a service for them.

Two particular needs assessment methods can be extremely useful in trying to determine the family needs in a community. These are not the only acceptable methods, but both get families involved in the needs assessment process. When these methods are used with the methods mentioned earlier (group dynamics, census data, national polls, local news media, etc.), a more accurate understanding of family needs can be obtained.

Because many churches try to minister to families in the church and also families in the community, a needs assessment method for each of these groups is suggested. A congregational questionnaire is one tool for assessing the needs of church families. The neighborhood interview is a tool for identifying needs of families in the community. However, interviews could be used with members of the congregation, and a survey could be distributed to the community. In some cases, a variety of needs assessment methods would be helpful, though not always feasible. The two following methods can be used by almost any church, and may be adequate for most churches.

Congregational Questionnaire

Appendix A contains a sample questionnaire that could be used to help assess the needs of families in your church. You have read through the questionnaire as part of exercise 3. The most important thing to remember is that *no* questionnaire is appropriate for use in *every* church. Your family life committee must discuss how to adapt the sample questionnaire for use in your congregation, and also whether this method is even appropriate.

As stated earlier, the needs assessment process can raise expectations for better family programs. If your family ministry committee is unable to meet these expectations, people may become apathetic toward family ministry. One of the ways to minimize this potential problem is to modify the sample questionnaire. If the family life committee feels that it is unable to provide some of the services listed in items 19 and 22 of the questionnaire, these services should not appear. Remember: for every item on the questionnaire, the family life committee should know how it can use the information to help plan timely, relevant, and practical programs.

Method of distribution is another key consideration. Questionnaires that are mailed (even when accompanied by a stamped, return envelope) usually have low return rates. Because the anonymity of respondents must be preserved, questionnaires cannot be distributed to small groups of individuals. One of the most effective ways to administer a questionnaire is at a general meeting of the congregation. Sunday worship is usually the time when the greatest proportion of the congregation is gathered together in one place, so administering the questionnaire during or after the worship assembly is probably the best time for most congregations.

Neighborhood Interviews

Family ministry is one way a church can serve the community. Family ministry can be an effective means to incorporate new families into the life of the church, but family ministry programs must be relevant to the felt needs of community members. Conducting a needs assessment of the congregation will not tell family ministry planners what needs exist in the community. To get an idea of how people in the community might respond to programs for families offered by the church, it is best to get people from the community involved in the needs assessment process.

(Note: If you are not sure why family ministry should extend beyond the members of the congregation, you may want to read ahead to chapter 7. Of course, community outreach should never replace family ministry within the church; a balance between the two is needed.)

Family needs in the community will not necessarily be the same as family needs of church members. Many of the needs of families in the church and community may be of serious or "crisis" proportions. You may also be surprised to find out that families in the community want to receive help in meeting the spiritual needs of their families. The point is that church leaders can't know what needs people in the community feel until they ask them. Through the process of needs assessment, church leaders will learn about particular needs in the community, and also how relevant current church programs are to those needs.

Conducting neighborhood interviews can be extremely informative. Through personal contact with people who live near the church and in the wider community, family ministry planners can plan programs which are relevant to actual needs. The interview itself demonstrates that the church is trying to be of service to the community. One of the primary reasons why people who call themselves Christians do not attend church is because they think religion is irrelevant to their daily problems. Reaching out to families in the community—asking people what their problems are—can be an important first step in letting people know the church cares.

Who should you interview? The answer depends on your community and whether your church has a special burden for a particular segment of the population. Some churches may want to begin their outreach to the community with certain groups of people, such as senior adults, low income families, or single parents. Or they may want to survey the people in the vicinity of the church building. Others may not know where to begin, so interviewing all types of people may help them decide whether or not to focus on families with special needs.

Once leaders in your church identify the types of families you want to help, you need to interview representative members of the target group. Selecting families at random is not always the best way to choose people to interview. A better way to find families which represent the diversity of family types in your community is to select particular types of families. For example, suppose that most people in your community live in single family residences. A random sample might lead you to interview 19 families in single family homes and 1 family living in an apartment. Selecting family types purposefully, on the other hand, may yield the following:

14 families living in single family residences;

1 family living in low income apartments;

2 families living in rural neighborhoods on the town outskirts;

2 families living in multiple family units such as duplexes or condominiums;

3 family members living in institutions such as nursing homes, foster care homes, or boarding houses.

Of course, identifying people by the type of home they live in is no guarantee that you will get a diversity of family types or ages. Other approaches can be used in addition to the one just suggested. You could interview people who have diverse occupations. It is relatively easy to find different family members who support their families through farming, manufacturing, sales, education, civil service, or providing professional services. Keeping a balance between men and women interviewed is also important.

Application Activities

1. What programs or services designed to enrich family life does your church currently offer to members of the community?

2. Do you feel your church ought to be doing more to reach out to non-Christian families?

Do you feel this outreach to non-Christians is a current priority, or does the church (and its family life committee) need to concentrate on other ministries first?

3. Read through the "Guide to Conducting a Neighborhood Interview" in appendix B.

Do you think conducting interviews in the community using interviews such as the guide suggests will help your committee better understand what needs for improved family living exist in your community?

If so, what types of families or family members (based on their residence or employment) do you think should be interviewed? Why?

What changes would you make in the interview guide to make it more appropriate to your community?

What plans, if any, do you think your committee should make to conduct such interviews in the community? (See appendix C)

What part, if any, are you willing to play in conducting the interviews?

Group Activities

Preparation for Group Meeting

Instructions for All Participants

Check off the following items as you prepare for the group meeting:

- ☐ *Read the chapter and complete the application activities.*
- ☐ *Look over the agenda for session 4.*
- ☐ *Make a note of any questions or comments you have about what you have read for this session (discuss them under agenda item 3).*
- ☐ *Write down your thoughts or reactions to the discussion questions suggested under agenda item 3.*
- ☐ *Pray about concerns you've become aware of through your preparation for this session.*

Leader's Instructions:

Preparation

- ☐ *Read the tips for session leaders (chapter 1).*
- ☐ *Read the chapter and the group activity agenda for session 4.*
- ☐ *Complete the exercises given in the chapter.*
- ☐ *Read all the leader's instructions (indicated in italics) before the meeting begins.*

Materials Needed

- ☐ *Newsprint, markers, masking tape.*

Group Meeting Agenda

1. Opening

- ☐ *If this study session is part of the regular meeting of a committee or class, check with the person in charge on the procedure for introducing this part of the meeting. Otherwise begin this session with prayer.*

2. Paired activity (10–15 minutes)

Divide the group into pairs, preferably pairing people who do not know each other very well.

Working independently, the first person in each pair answers the following questions for himself or herself. He should place a "1," "2," or "3" next to the three items which currently have the highest priority or need in his or her life.

Then the second member of each pair tries to guess how the first person would answer, in effect, "assessing" his or her needs.

- ☐ *I need a haircut or a different hair style.*
- ☐ *I need to learn how to shop more wisely for food.*
- ☐ *I need a refresher course on home maintenance.*
- ☐ *I need a new pair of dress shoes.*
- ☐ *I need a course on interior decorating.*
- ☐ *I need to check the oil in my car more often.*
- ☐ *g.I need to learn a new hobby.*

- ☐ *I need to keep better track of current events.*
- ☐ *I need to buy a new refrigerator.*
- ☐ *I need to watch less television.*
- ☐ *I need to take voice lessons.*
- ☐ *I need to write letters more frequently to distant friends.*

How accurate were the second members of each pair?

How did the people whose needs were "assessed" feel?

What can we learn from this activity about the dangers of assessing others' needs without involving them in the process?

- ☐ *People who are paired together do not need to sit together.*
- ☐ *Be clear which person is the first member of the pair and which is the second.*
- ☐ *After allowing a few minutes for ranking the needs, move on to discuss the last three questions in the activity.*

3. Large group discussion (20–25 minutes)

- ☐ *Have the group discuss all 5 questions.*
- ☐ *In addition, at this time individuals may bring up questions or comments they had about the chapter for consideration by the entire group.*

Discussion topics:

1. Is it appropriate to conduct a needs assessment of the congregation at the present time? Why or why not?
2. Is it appropriate to conduct a needs assessment of family needs in the community at the present time? Why or why not?
3. Do we want to plan to use a modified version of the sample questionnaire for the congregational needs assessment? How will we modify it?
4. Do we want to use neighborhood interviews for the assessment of community family needs? (See appendix C)
5. What other methods for needs assessment should we consider?

- ☐ *newspaper articles (compare exercise 2,.)*
- ☐ *surveys, polls, census data*
- ☐ *key informant interviews*

4. Small group activity (20–25 minutes)

If the answers to questions 1, 2, 3, and 4 were "no," remain in a large group and discuss when a needs assessment will be done, and whether either of the two methods should be considered later.

If the answer to either question 3 or 4 was "no," remain in a large group. Develop a plan for using the method that was chosen (questionnaire or interviews). How will it be used, who will do it, how will it be done, who will compile the results?

If the answers to both questions 3 and 4 were "yes," divide into two groups. Each group develop a plan for using one of the methods (one group plans to use the questionnaire, the other plans to use the interviews). Then form one large group and share the plans. Discuss and modify the plans as needed. If possible, approve the two plans.

- ☐ *If two groups are formed, allow people to choose whichever small group they wish. The two small groups do not have to be the same size.*
- ☐ *If time does not allow the group to come to a consensus about what will be done, schedule another opportunity for the group to meet and discuss these issues.*
- ☐ *Emphasize that when the plan(s) to use the questionnaire and/or*

interviews are approved, group members must commit themselves to carrying out the plans. Results of the needs assessment should be tabulated and made available to group members by session 9.

5. Closing and prayer

- ☐ *Ask for a volunteer to lead the next group meeting.*
- ☐ *Close in prayer.*

NOTES

"[From the New Testament we can conclude that] there is clearly a kindly, personal relating in the church. A corporate superficial expression of love and responsibility cannot possibly qualify for the intimate expressions of the church family seen in the New Testament. All of the close, dynamic aspects of family life are to be found in the church body: cherishing, caring, encouraging, rebuking, confessing, repenting, confronting, forgiving, expressing kindness and communicating honestly. . . .

Church life and family life are closely interrelated in New Testament experience. The dynamic relationship between the two is so obvious that it appears to be taken for granted by the New Testament writers."

Charles Sell, *Family Ministry*, p. 79

Chapter 5
Toward a Biblical Foundation for Family Ministry

Family In The Bible

In this chapter we focus on the biblical foundation for a ministry to families. This subject is important—if we can't biblically back up what we are doing as Bible-believing Christians, we have problems. However, if we *do* find biblical justification and *don't* do something we also have problems. This chapter contains a foundation on which to build our family ministry.

As mentioned in the last chapter, we will discuss families on two levels. One level deals with the care and enrichment of our own Christian families. The other level deals with families in the community. The two levels of ministry complement each other and should be pursued together.

Though the word "family" is used in the Old Testament 250 times, the word seldom occurs in any English translation of the New Testament. Yet, we see all the major truths of God's Word in relation to the concepts of family and family relationships. Like a brightly colored thread woven into the Scriptures, God establishes the family as the basic human institution created and ordained by Him.

If we had no concept of family relationships, we would have difficulty understanding such basic ideas as the fatherhood of God, our adoption as children of God, or fellowship with Christian brothers and sisters. The Bible gives us specific principles to apply to family ministry (such as loving and bearing with one another) but also places the family at the very core of what it means to be human in God's world.

Theological Principles

In the remainder of this chapter, we will consider seven reasons why God and His Word are concerned about family life—and why His church should also be concerned.

1 God chose the analogy of the family to reveal himself to mankind.

Of all the analogies known to man, God chose the concept of "father," in its purest and finest sense, to convey His relationship to mankind. Jesus Christ is described as the Only Begotten "Son" of God. The church is pictured by Paul as the "bride" of Christ. We are "brothers and sisters," another family analogy. The institution of marriage is the first interpersonal relationship established by God (Gen. 2:23–24). In Ephesians 5:21–33, Paul shows the close analogy between Christ and His church and the husband-wife relationship. God in His wisdom believed people could best understand His nature and His relationship to creation through family roles.

2 Jesus was concerned about family relationships and about meeting human needs.

To the demon-possessed man Jesus said, "Go home to your family and tell them how much the Lord has done for you, and how He has had mercy on you" (Mark 5:18). To the widow of Nain Jesus said, "Don't cry" (Luke 7:13). Luke records that His heart went out to her at the death of her only son. "God has come to help His people" (Luke 7:16), the crowd shouted. The list could go on and on—Jesus healing Peter's mother-in-law, helping lepers rejoin their families, healing sick children, restoring sight and hearing. All these people were members of families who had experienced great anxiety and loss.

Consider Jesus' parable of the Sheep and the Goats in Matthew 25. In the first part of the parable, Jesus commends His faithful followers for responding to others in need—whether their need was physical (hunger, thirst, lack of clothes, sickness) or social (hospitality, visitation).

> *For I was hungry and you gave Me something to eat, I was thirsty and you gave Me something to drink, I was a stranger and you invited Me in, I needed clothes and you clothed me, I was sick and you looked after Me, I was in prison and you came to visit Me (Matt. 25:35-36).*

In each case, a human need was met. Who are "the least of these brothers" if they are not the people we come into contact with every day? Jesus is not talking about people we never meet. He's talking about ministering to the needs of people we see frequently.

What about the people *you* see every day? Do they have family needs? Do they need to learn more effective ways of relating to their spouses or children or parents or in-laws? Are most of their families hurting and in trouble? Our response should be to let Jesus work through us by showing His compassion for the family needs of others.

Application Activities

1. What principles are taught in the following Scripture passages which suggest the importance of family relationships?

Rise in the presence of the aged, show respect for the elderly, and revere your God. I am the Lord (Lev. 19:32).

If a man has recently married, he must not be sent to war or have any other duty laid on him. For one year he is to be free to stay at home and bring happiness to the wife he has married (Deut. 24:5).

"Look," said Naomi, "your sister-in-law is going back to her people and her gods. Go back with her." But Ruth replied, "Don't urge me to leave you or turn back from you. Where you go I will go, and where you stay I will stay. Your people will be my people and your God my God" (Ruth 1:15–16).

My son, keep your father's commands and do not forsake your mother's teaching. Bind them on your hearts forever; fasten them around your neck. When you walk, they will guide you; when you sleep, they will watch over you; when you awake, they will speak to you. For these commands are a lamp, this teaching is a light, and the corrections of discipline are the way to life (Prov. 6:20–23).

Do not let any unwholesome talk come out of your mouths, but only what is helpful for building others up according to their needs, that it may benefit those who listen (Eph. 4:29).

Bear with each other and forgive whatever grievances you may have against one another. Forgive as the Lord forgave you (Col. 3:13).

More Principles for Ministry

We are looking at reasons why God is concerned about families and why churches should also be concerned.

A third principle can be stated as follows:

3 The Bible views people as whole people living their lives in relation to others; therefore family ministry must be integrated into all areas of a person's life.

The Hebrew concept of the unity of each person (from which the New Testament view of man is derived) forbids us to minister to "spiritual" needs alone while excluding other needs. True, the fundamental problem of all human beings is spiritual, but the symptoms of our spiritual disease—sin—also affects us physically, psychologically, and socially.

We are aware of the close connection between one's physical problems and his or her emotional conditions. The Bible's wholistic view of man should remind us that when family problems exist, they can cause spiritual problems and even physical ailments within the family.

The church's response to this wholistic view of people should be a ministry to families that takes into account their spiritual, emotional, physical, and social conditions. Family members profoundly affect one another. When one member has problems of any kind, other family members are usually affected in some way.

Family ministry cannot be confined to cognitive forms of ministry alone. Educating people about biblical ideals and practical tips for family living doesn't always fulfill family needs. Sometimes telling people what they ought to be doing only makes them feel guilty because they can't live up to someone else's standard. Those who carry out a family ministry must be ready to get involved in every aspect of people's day-to-day struggles, be willing to befriend others, and be able to feel the hurt of brothers and sisters in Christ. Family ministry can never be reduced to a prescription for what ails people. It must always take the form of Christ living in us.

The fourth reason churches need to be involved in family ministry is:

4 The stability of the church depends on the stability of families.

The Bible teaches that the family is the laboratory for Christian living. If it doesn't work at home, where does it work? The biblical admonitions about interpersonal relationships (e.g., Ephesians 4:29–32 and 1 Corinthians 13:4–7) apply to our family relationships as much as they do to our relationships with others. It is a shame when we treat total strangers with more courtesy and respect than we do those of our own households.

Notice Paul's admonition to Timothy about the characteristics of the leaders of the church. In 1 Timothy 3:4 Paul says, "He must manage his own family well and see that his children obey him with proper respect." Paul then adds a penetrating question that reveals his intense concern about this important trait: "If anyone does not know how to manage his own family, how can he take care of God's church?" (v.5)

The home is the laboratory for Christian living. The New Testament emphasizes the development of family life. A church with strong families will be a strong church.

Application Activities

1. Family problems cannot always be put into neat little compartments. In cases of divorce one family member may be morally rebelling against God and be the root cause of a particular family problem. But the results of divorce are many and complex—affecting every area of life. Family needs cannot be reduced to only spiritual needs or only physical needs or only social needs. Yet family ministry programs often neglect one or more aspects of family life.

EXAMPLE: Consider the case of a couple with children where the father loses his job. The immediate family needs are *physical*—how will they pay for food, clothing, and shelter? Soon both parents and children face *emotional* stresses and uncertainties about the future. The family's *social* life and needs change, friends and neighbors relate to them differently—sometimes awkwardly as if from pity, sometimes out of genuine care and concern. The family members have *mental* needs—the father may need to learn a new trade or vocation, the mother may need to learn new coping skills; the children may need to learn to go without an allowance. *Spiritually,* the family's circumstances may help draw them closer together as they trust God to provide for their needs. Or it may have the opposite effect. A program designed to help families of the unemployed must consider all the dimensions of this problem.

Choose *one* of the following family problems or situations. Identify or describe some of the particular consequences of that problem and what different needs these families might have.

Families with handicapped children
Families with an alcoholic parent
Special needs of single parents
Special needs of the widowed

Physical needs:

Social needs:

Emotional needs:

Mental or learning needs:

Moral and spiritual needs:

2. First Timothy 3:4 says, "He [the overseer] must manage his own family well and see that his children obey him with proper respect." The following five statements are opinions of how this verse might be applied in the local church. No statement is necessarily right or wrong. How do you feel about these opinions? Circle your response following each statement.

SA—strongly agree

A —agree

N —No opinion

D —disagree

SD—strongly disagree

"The church isn't perfect, and neither are church leaders. All of us are sinners and suffer the consequences of sin even though we are forgiven. Church leaders are bound to have family problems. If God forgives them, why shouldn't the church?"

SA A N D SD

"It's one thing to be a good parent. But there is only so much you can do. Sooner or later kids grow up, and some of them will rebel. It's not the parents' fault. Parents aren't responsible for the actions of their children."

SA A N D SD

"It depends on the position a person holds. If he manages the church, it doesn't matter what kind of family life he has."

SA A N D SD

"When kids go wrong, it's not the parents' fault. But it still sets a bad example for the rest of the church. A person in a leadership position should step down if family trouble arises."

SA A N D SD

"Sometimes you have to go through a trial yourself to be able to help someone else who's going through it. How can someone who has never been divorced really understand someone who is going through one? So we need people who have suffered family problems to be in leadership positions in a family ministry."

SA A N D SD

Is divorce an issue in your church? If so, pray for the people involved. Pray for healing in the families affected. Pray for wisdom for church leaders who must decide what to do. In the space below, write any other thoughts you have on this issue.

Family Ministry and The Church

The last three reasons why family ministry should be important in a church are that family ministry is an effective way for the church to: worship God, be the community of His people, and reach out to a lost world.

5 Family ministry is an effective means to help families worship God.

If the family is the laboratory for living the Christian life, then worship should be the center of each family's life together. If our chief end is to glorify God, then living to bring honor and praise to our Creator must begin in the home.

Corporate public worship—the time when the entire church gathers to celebrate who God is and what He has done for us—is a central part of any church's life. But worship does not begin and end with the formal worship service. We come to the service already worshiping, we join in worship with others, and when we leave, we continue to worship God privately. The Christian home should be an environment which fosters praise. It is in day-to-day living that we experience God's love through our family members and respond in thanksgiving to Him. At key points in the family cycle—births and birthdays, marriages and anniversaries, and at death—we are reminded of God's gifts of life and family.

One way a family ministry fosters true family worship is by helping parents take responsibility for the moral training of their children. Family devotions are important, but family worship goes beyond a set time and place for Bible reading, song, and prayer. As a family ministry touches individual lives with the healing power of the Gospel, family members find new reasons to praise God together.

6 Family ministry is an effective means of helping Christians build each other up in love.

Family ministry means helping individual families grow together. That involves helping individuals better live their roles in the family. Family ministry also means helping different families grow together. As families learn to appreciate and help one another, the entire church body is knit together in a closer bond of fellowship.

What can be more edifying to the church and more glorifying to God than for families to learn how to enrich the quality of their lives together? Another aspect of edification is using Christian volunteers to work in family ministry programs. Volunteers exercise a variety of spiritual gifts as they teach, counsel, and encourage fellow Christians.

7 A family ministry is an effective means of outreach in the community.

Christians are called on to be salt, light, and leaven in a chaotic world. The church is faced with a decision—to talk to itself and spend money on itself or to accept Jesus' challenge to make a difference in the lives of people. A ministry to families is one good way to be involved as salt and leaven and light in your community. Many Christians have taken the ministry to families seriously and found community people open and receptive.

Church growth experts tell us that the most effective way to evangelize is through family relationships. A ministry to families then is not an optional fringe program that we might pursue as a church. It is the center of what it means to be Christ's church.

Evangelism possibilities are tremendous. People willingly respond to the claims of the Gospel when they see that Christians genuinely care about their individual and family problems. People appreciate a church willing to show its faith in a way that benefits family life. The family enrichment emphasis is of high interest and low controversy, thus helping to break down religious prejudices.

Perhaps a word of warning is in order. A meaningful program of family ministry to the community may be hazardous to your "status quo." But an examination of Jesus' ministry reveals the direction our ministry should take, if we take discipleship seriously. Physicians go where sick people are.

Application Activities

1. Family ministry can be an effective way to encourage family worship. Write down one practical way families could be helped to worship more together through an existing ministry in your church.

2. Family ministry can be an effective way to promote better fellowship among family members. Write down one practical way family members could be helped to build each other up through an existing ministry in your church.

3. Family ministry can be an effective way to reach out into the community. In an earlier chapter, the following were identified as current social problems:

alcoholism
drug abuse
spouse abuse
divorce
suicide
teenage pregnancy
child abuse
homosexuality

Choose one of these problems. Then suggest one practical way your church might be able to help family members in the community who are affected by this problem.

Group Activities

Preparation for Group Meeting

Instructions for All Participants

Check off the following items as you prepare for the group meeting:

- ☐ *Read the chapter and complete the application activities.*
- ☐ *Look over the agenda for session 5.*
- ☐ *Make a note of any questions or comments you have about what you have read for this session (discuss them under agenda item 4).*
- ☐ *Write down your thoughts or reactions to the discussion questions suggested under agenda item 4.*

- ☐ Pray about concerns you've become aware of through your preparation for this session.

Leader's Instructions:

Preparation

- ☐ *Read the tips for session leaders (chapter 1).*
- ☐ *Read the chapter and the group activity agenda for session 5.*
- ☐ *Complete the exercises given in the chapter.*
- ☐ *Read all the leader's instructions (indicated in italics) before the meeting begins.*

Materials Needed

- ☐ *Newsprint, markers, masking tape.*

Group Meeting Agenda

1. Opening

- ☐ *If this study session is part of the regular meeting of a committee or class, check with the person in charge on the procedure for introducing this part of the meeting. Otherwise begin this session with prayer.*

2. Small group activity (15–20 minutes)

Purpose: to observe in the life of Jesus characteristics that reveal how He related to people as He ministered to them—in order that we might be more like Him.

Task: Examine one of the following passages and identify ways Jesus helped people—how He was sensitive to their needs, how He responded to their requests for help, how He restored them and their relationships to others.

Passages:

Matt. 19:16–30	(the rich young man)
Mark 2:1–12	(healing of a paralytic)
Luke 7:11–17	(Jesus raises a widow's son)
Luke 19:1–10	(Jesus and Zacchaeus)
John 4:4–26	(the Samaritan woman)
John 9:1–12	(Jesus heals a blind man)

- ☐ *Divide the group into several small groups of 4–5 people per group.*
- ☐ *Ask the members of each small group to briefly discuss which passage they would like to examine. Have each group examine a different passage, unless there are more than six small groups.*
- ☐ *Each group should have a recorder and reporter for sharing with the large group.*
- ☐ *Give the groups 15–20 minutes to make their observations.*

3. Share ideas with the large group (10 minutes)

- ☐ *Ask the reporter for each group to share its ideas and observations about Jesus' style of helping people.*
- ☐ *After the ideas are presented, you may want to allow time for comments or questions from members of other small groups.*

4. Large group discussion (20–25 minutes)

- ☐ *Ask the group which topics listed below they would like to discuss.*
- ☐ *In addition, at this time individuals may bring up questions or comments they had about the chapter.*

Discussion topics:

1. How do family concerns today differ from those in Jesus' time? How are they the same? How would Jesus respond to the needs of families today?

2 What kind of family life example should church leaders be required to have? (Refer to application activity 3 and the different opinions reflected there.)

3 "People need people, but they don't necessarily have to be blood relatives. The traditional notion of family is changing and may eventually die out. But people will find other ways to have needs met. Perhaps the church will be a partial replacement for the family." Do you agree or disagree? Discuss.

5. The importance of family (large group activity) (5-10 minutes)

List reasons why the family—a gift given to all people in all times—is important in God's plan for His church and for the world.

- ☐ *Concisely write the reasons why the family is important. Use newsprint or a chalkboard.*
- ☐ *You will want to keep the reasons suggested and distribute them for future reference.*

6. Closing and prayer

- ☐ *Ask for a group member to volunteer to lead the next group meeting.*
- ☐ *Close in prayer.*

NOTES

"The literature that is important in understanding how families change over time is the literature on the life cycle of the family. . . . What is needed is a strategy for preventive family life education in the church that provokes families to anticipate the demands of the approaching stage in the life cycle as well as provides support during their present stage."

Dennis Guernsey, *A New Design for Family Ministry*, p. 42

Chapter 6
Practical Foundations of Family Ministry—Part 1

Our Task

Hopefully you are convinced that something *can* and *should* be done in your church to develop a better ministry to families. What is the next step? Remember family ministry is not something you start or add to your regular church program. It already exists to some degree and needs to be integrated throughout everything the church does.

We *can* strengthen and improve family ministry. Our task in this chapter and the next is to lay down some practical foundations for family ministry so that your church will be able to improve the quality and quantity of family services. It's like adding additional floors to an already-existing building. The contractor must first be sure that the present foundation can withstand the weight and stress of an addition. To use Jesus' terms in Luke 6:48, we want to be sure that we lay our foundation for family ministry on rock.

We are often tempted to start programs and activities in random fashion out of our enthusiasm and concern for families. This directionless, short-sighted foundation only lasts temporarily. All ministries are built on a set of assumptions. Everything the church does has underlying theological and practical assumptions. Careful builders (i.e. church leaders) spend much time planning and becoming aware of the far-reaching implications of what is to take place so that when "floods" strike the foundation, it will provide strong support.

A carpenter can build two identical-looking houses—one on rock and the other on sand—the only difference is their foundations. Let's look at some practical foundations of family ministry that will insure stability and give it direction, purpose, and continuity.

A Wholistic Approach

1 *Family ministry should be wholistic in approach.*

Your church needs to look at the whole spectrum of family ministry. This approach is conceptualized in the form of a circle with four parts. It can be illustrated as follows:

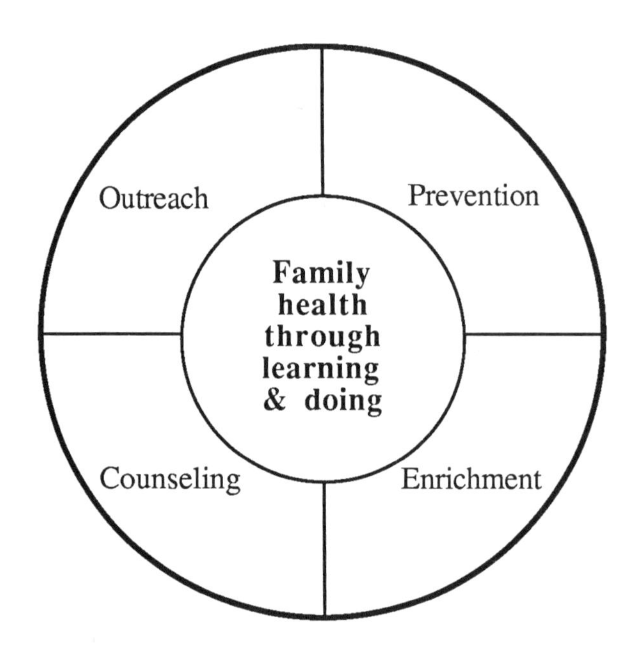

Learning and doing

At the center of the diagram is family health through learning and doing. Everything the church offers to families is designed to promote better family health. All family ministry programs help people *learn* about themselves and their families and *act* upon what they learn. Individual church programs may focus on family enrichment or the management of family crises, but essentially we want people to learn new ways of behaving together as a family and new ways of looking at themselves as a family unit. **The ultimate goal is the *health* of the family: physical, emotional, social, mental, and spiritual.**

Prevention

The cry from church leaders is, "What can we do to stop family disintegration in our churches?" The answer is not simply to train more Christian counselors. Something must be done to get ahead of the problem, to address it before it gets to unmanageable proportions. It makes the most sense to equip families with necessary skills to deal with issues effectively *before* they develop into full-blown crises.

The goal of prevention is to transmit effective problem-solving techniques and conflict resolution skills that will help defuse negative family communication. One common problem in conflict situations is that neither party listens. It is impossible to listen to another person and formulate a response at the same time. With this approach, the conflict intensifies. The way a person words a difference, the tone of voice, setting, and timing of the encounter also affect the outcome of a conflict. Skills can be taught to increase the probability of successful conflict resolution. Conflict *can* be a blessing and growth experience for those who know how to handle it.

Big marital and family problems have small beginnings. The Bible has much to say about how to get along with one another—an effective family ministry reflects that emphasis.

We must keep our primary goal in focus—to keep marriages and families together by providing positive opportunities for growth, strength, and wellness. An ounce of prevention is worth a ton of cure!

What about offering evening classes to the public on such topics as preparation for marriage, family communication, parenting, single living, etc.? Support groups can be organized to meet periodically with people who have special needs. For example, widows, divorcees, or single parents, can come together for mutual upbuilding under the leadership of qualified, mature Christians. Through these meetings, Christians can make contact with community people. This interaction may encourage non-Christians to become part of the family of God.

Enrichment

Preventing major problems from occurring is not enough; we need to promote positive and enriching family experiences. The church should offer a wide range of activities that families can participate in as a "family" and which strengthen their family relationships. Such activities or programs may be oriented toward recreation, service, learning, or worship. Examples include all-church picnics, family retreats, mother-daughter banquets, community outreach projects, walk-through-the-Bible seminars, and emphases on special days such as Mother's Day or Father's Day.

Programs can be designed to involve and serve the older members of the church and community. Volunteers could be organized to assist senior citizens with matters involving Social Security, food stamps, Medicare, housing, income tax, nursing needs, etc. This often-neglected age-group can be a tremendous blessing. At another age-level, think of the good things that could result from interaction with families with new babies in your area. Such community involvement gives Christians an opportunity to share the various church ministries with families who are probably more vulnerable spiritually than at any other time in their lives.

Counseling

Our overall emphasis is on prevention and enrichment, but provision has to be made for family and individual counseling. A church that has an active outreach in the community will find families under extreme stress or in crisis situations who need outside assistance. There will also be other people (from the church and the community) who participate in the preventive-oriented programs of the church, and need individual attention to their problems. Churches involved in family ministries have an obligation to see that counseling needs are met. Churches can provide the services themselves or make sure they are provided through adequate referral services. There may be opportunities to use trained volunteer counselors willing to minister in this much-needed way.

Outreach

This emphasis is particularly applicable to people in the community who become a part of our church's family ministry. My remarks here are primarily about those people who are not Christians. Various programs of family ministry provide an excellent way for community people to be introduced to Christians and to the Christian faith. In a warm and accepting environment, they can learn the blessings of the Christian life as they hear it taught and see it lived in the family-related activities.

We must be careful not to take undue advantage of people or misrepresent what we are attempting to do in our ministry to families. Nevertheless, we should be constantly aware of the need to share the saving Gospel of Christ with individuals and families who have that spiritual need.

In one sense, evangelism should permeate every aspect of our ministry to those who are not Christians. It is included in a separate section of our diagram for purposes of emphasis.

The content of these areas varies according to individual congregational and community needs. But a comprehensive Christian ministry to families includes all four elements and also promotes the health and wellbeing of families.

Application Activities

1. The following list contains a number of preventive programs that could possibly be sponsored by your church. First read through the list carefully.

☐ Preparation for Marriage

☐ Marriage Enrichment

☐ Parent Training (dual and single)

☐ People Helping (training people for involvement)

☐ Family Communication

☐ Planning Family Together Times

☐ Family Financial Planning

☐ Building Self-Esteem in the Family

☐ Parent Training in Sex Education

☐ Drug and Alcohol Abuse

☐ Coping with Terminal Illness, Death, and Grief

☐ Helping our Aging Parents

☐ Mid-Life Issues: Crisis or Transition?

☐ Pre-Retirement and Retirement

☐ Abundant Single Living

☐ The Family Clan: In-Laws or Outlaws?

---

a. Which topics has your congregation covered in the last two years in a class or seminar setting?

---

b. Go back and mark the top three topics (1, 2, 3) you feel need to be covered within the coming year.

---

c. What format do you think might be best for each topic (midweek service, Sunday Bible class, weekend retreat, evening series, etc.)?

1

2

3

d. Can you think of other topics that would be good to offer?

1

2

3

2. For each of the following enrichment programs, list at least one family activity that is needed or would be well-received in your church.

Family enrichment through:

____
Recreation

____
Service

____
Learning

____
Worship

____
(other)

Ups and Downs of Family Life

2 The ministry should be developed with an awareness of the transition and crisis points in the family life cycle.

Every person goes through a series of definite, somewhat predictable stages of growth and experiences. At first, childhood stages of development were identified by developmental psychologists. In the last decade, increased attention has been given to identifying the stages adults go through. Each adult stage also has unique characteristics and problems.

The traditional adult transition points usually begin with the pre-marital stage—forming of love commitment to another person. Early marriage follows, with its combination of euphoria, optimism, and naivety. By the time two have become one in marriage and settled down to the reality of living, they often become three, maybe more. The developmental stage of parenting has distinct characteristics, putting added responsibilities and new strains on the marital relationship.

The challenging and somewhat trying times of parenting adolescents comes next—equipping teens to leave the home with minimal damaging effects on the home (and other family members). Suddenly they are gone, and the home is empty. This stage is critical for many married couples. Husband and wife are back together—just the two of them. The quality of the marriage reflects the attention they spent on their relationship through the years.

The retirement years follow, bringing a new set of problems. In time, one of the spouses will die, leaving the other to face yet another major life adjustment.

With some variation, this family life cycle is repeated by most families. The point is this—*people are usually more vulnerable to some type of outside assistance during transition and crisis points.*

An effective family ministry must incorporate these findings. We need to develop programs in our churches that equip adults to cope successfully with these transition points. Whether or not adults are prepared before and during these changes determines if the event will be a transition or a crisis.

Application Activities

1. How many of the following adult family transition points have you experienced?

☐ Pre-marriage

☐ Early Marriage

☐ Parenting

☐ Adolescent Parenting

☐ Empty Nest

☐ Retirement

☐ Death of Spouse

Choose any two of the family transition points. List them in the left-hand column. In the middle column, write down the key struggles of this developmental stage. For example, in retirement, the use of one's leisure time and one's attitude toward saving and spending money are areas of major change. In the right-hand column, write down how the church could help people cope with those particular struggles.

Transition Points	Key Struggles	Helpful Ideas

To better understand the stages of family transition, you may want to interview a retired or widowed person from your church.

No Family Is an Island . . .

3 The development of a strong social support system needs to be emphasized.

A "social support system" refers to the role that people outside the immediate family play as they relate to the family. Research on family stress revealed that families who have strong support systems (neighborhood, friends, church, etc.) can withstand almost any crisis. Death of a family member, moving, career change, or loss of job, are crises that are absorbed in part by caring, supportive friends.

Family specialists emphasize the importance of meaningful social contacts for families. Yet we know that many families today are isolated and lonely, cut off from their relatives and friends by distance, and have no one to fill the void.

Churches need to concentrate on uniting isolated families with other people. The church should minister to people who are separated from one another and who do not have all the support they need within their own families.

People desperately need community life as well as a rewarding family life. We must provide community life and meaningful fellowship for Christian families. That is part of being the family of God. The church is in an ideal position to provide authentic social support for its members.

Application Activities

1. Who are the "neglected people" in your church—those who have little or no support system and who don't seem to fit into any group?

a. What can you do to make these people feel more a part of the church family?

b. What do the following verses say that can help us with this problem?

Therefore, as we have opportunity, let us do good to all people, especially to those who belong to the family of believers (Gal. 6:10).

My brothers, as believers in our glorious Lord Jesus Christ, don't show favoritism (James 2:1).

If you really keep the royal law found in Scripture, "Love your neighbor as yourself," you are doing right. But if you show favoritism, you sin and are convicted by the law as lawbreakers (James 2:8–9).

But when you give a banquet, invite the poor, the crippled, the lame, the blind, and you will be blessed. Although they cannot repay you, you will be repaid at the resurrection of the righteous (Luke 14:13–14).

Offer hospitality to one another without grumbling (1 Peter 4:9).

In Step with the Times

4 Family ministry should be contemporary and realistic.

Modern families are greatly influenced by industrialization and technology. They live in a fast-paced world and struggle to find creative answers to their problems. The church's task is to make biblical truth relevant to the contemporary family's circumstances. Simply being "relevant" is not our goal. It is a necessary way of influencing people with eternal biblical truths so they can experience the fullness of life—including the family life that God intends for them (John 10:10). Modern people do not respond to a message or method that they feel is outdated and irrelevant.

Contemporary people struggle with the meaning of life. Emptiness, loneliness, and a lack of purpose plague modern man. Issues such as abortion, old age, and the threat of a nuclear holocaust have a common question running through them—how sacred and meaningful is life? God's Word has the ultimate answer to the searching questions of a confused society.

Being contemporary requires a realistic view of where families are and what problems they face. Family ministry must deal with frustrations as well as joys, failures as well as successes, conflict as well as harmony. All families face these—even the best Christian families. There are no easy solutions to the complicated struggles faced by today's families. But our ministry to families should reflect a true picture of reality.

Application Activities

1. The following eight sentences describe different forms of stress placed on modern families. Some are more significant than others, but all describe trends which prevail today.

For each one, identify one experience in your own life that illustrates the tension between modern life and commitment to family.

Next, select two of the statements. For each one, list two or more ways your church could be more relevant to the needs of families today through its family ministry.

________________________________ *a.* The day-to-day activities of individuals are associated more and more with *impersonal institutions*—employer, schools, health-care facilities, banks, merchants—than with family members or neighbors.

________________________________ *b.* Life in the *city* holds more attractions than life in the country—better jobs, living conditions, cultural activities—but city life separates families from each other.

________________________________ *c.* Our views and images of the world are not shaped by people we know and trust—family members, friends, our ministers—but by the *mass media.*

________________________________ *d.* Though *technology* could be used to give us more time to spend with our families, we actually spend less. We end up spending more time acquiring, using, repairing, and replacing all the technological gadgets that were supposed to make life easier.

e. *Time* is no longer used to experience relationships, to live in community, to enjoy working and playing. Instead, time is to be mastered and used efficiently. We live by the minute and second hands of our wristwatches. Family is often scheduled right out of our lives.

f. Focus has shifted from the group and the family to the *individual.* "Find self-fulfillment above all else"—we are told.

g. The modern world is a world full of *options* for the individual. The ties to tradition and family values no longer exist.

h. Modern life is increasingly *secular.* God and religious meaning are divorced from every aspect of life: work, government, art, knowledge, health, the home.

All Things to All Families

5 Family ministry must reach a variety of family types.

Traditionally the word "family," when used within the church context, meant a husband, his one and only wife, and their children—the nuclear family. The wife was usually not employed outside the home. Today the key word to describe the American family is "change." The nuclear family as just described accounts for somewhere between 15 and 30 percent of the American population—that includes dual career couples. And the percentage is dropping steadily. The number of single people, married people with no children, single-parent families, and step-families is increasing.

In the past most churches reacted to the changing family structure with indifference or rejection. In recent years, the trend has been to recognize a variety of family forms. If the church holds a strong theological stance that is pro-marriage and anti-divorce and affirms the value of human life, most family forms can be recognized. An effective family ministry must take into account the needs of an increasing variety of family types.

Application Activities

1. How would you describe the various types of families found in your church? Briefly describe (in short phrases) as many different family types found in your church.

There is no correct number of family types—you may have anywhere from four or five to ten or more. Examples might include:

Married couples with no children
Divorced men, not remarried

What percentage of families in your church do you think would fall in each of these categories? (Make sure they add up to 100 percent.)

Are there other types of families in your community that are not represented in your church? List these.

Group Activities

Preparation for Group Meeting

Instructions for All Participants

Check off the following items as you prepare for the group meeting:

- ☐ *Read the chapter and complete the application activities.*
- ☐ *Look over the agenda for session 6.*
- ☐ *Write down your thoughts about the group tasks under agenda item 2.*
- ☐ *Pray about concerns you've become aware of while preparing for this session.*

Leader's Instructions:

Preparation

- ☐ *Read the tips for session leaders (chapter 1).*
- ☐ *Read the chapter and the group activity agenda for session 6.*
- ☐ *Complete the exercises given in the chapter.*
- ☐ *Read all the leader's instructions (indicated in italics) before the meeting begins.*

Materials Needed

- ☐ *Newsprint, markers, masking tape, chalkboard, chalk.*

Group Meeting Agenda

1. Opening

- ☐ *If this study session is part of the regular meeting of a committee or class, check with the person in charge on the procedure for introducing this part of the meeting. Otherwise begin this session with prayer.*

2. Small group activity (20–25 minutes)

Two groups will each outline a plan to implement a specific, family-oriented program, as follows:

- ☐ *Group one: Marriage enrichment program*
- ☐ *Group two: Single parenting program*

Each group should outline the basic steps it would take to plan their program. These steps should include:

- ☐ *identifying broad objectives for the program*
- ☐ *describing what content needs to be included*
- ☐ *suggesting how families will be involved*

A recorder from each group should write on newsprint the general activities that the group would do to carry out its family ministry program. Remember: group members are only *outlining* a plan for a family program. Details needs not be included.

Group members should follow as many of the foundational principles given in this session as possible:

- ☐ *be preventive in nature*
- ☐ *follow transition and crisis points in the family life cycle*
- ☐ *develop a strong social support system*
- ☐ *be contemporary and realistic*
- ☐ *reach a variety of family types.*

A reporter from each group should be prepared to explain *why* (in terms of the five principles—or other principles) the group would take the steps listed on the newsprint.

- ☐ *Divide the large group into two smaller groups. The two groups do not have to be the same size.*
- ☐ *Remind the groups that this is a learning activity and the proposed programs aren't expected to be perfect.*
- ☐ *Notify group members five minutes and two minutes before the allotted time period is up.*

3. Share program plans with large group (20–30 minutes)

The recorder and/or reporter from the small groups explains the group's family ministry program—giving a brief rationale for each part of the plan.

Following each presentation, members of the other small group may ask questions or give comments (5–7 minutes). When reacting to the proposed program, group members should pay particular attention to the five principles for family ministry given in the guided-study article.

- ☐ *Have one group present its plan (5–10 minutes), then allow discussion (5–7 minutes). Repeat the procedure with the other small group, leaving time at the end of the meeting for agenda item 4.*
- ☐ *Encourage group members to be creative in suggesting ways the programs could be structured to include the foundational principles. It is less important that every aspect of the plans be completely workable.*

4. Summary (10 minutes) What recommendations would you make to church leaders as they plan for family ministry? Be specific.

- ☐ *Record suggestions on a chalkboard or newsprint.*

5. Closing and prayer

- ☐ *Ask for a group member to volunteer to lead the next group meeting.*
- ☐ *Close in prayer.*

NOTES

“If we preach a gospel that neglects the welfare of the whole in exchange for the happiness of the individual, then the Church as a living, pulsing body is weakened as is the welfare of the family. We must recover the priority of interrelationships.”

Dennis Guernsey, *A New Design for Family Ministry,* p. 99

Chapter 7
Practical Foundations of Family Ministry—Part 2

Review

In the last chapter, we talked about the necessity of laying down some practical foundations of family ministry in order for church leaders to improve the quality and increase the quantity of family-oriented services. All ministries are built on certain assumptions, so it is important that we identify and evaluate them. In the previous session, practical foundations of family ministry were listed. In this session we examine six additional concepts to consider in designing a family ministry.

Family: More Than Individuals

*6 **A family needs to be viewed as a system rather than as a group of separate individuals.***

The family operates as a system. In any system what affects one member also affects the rest of the members. The family unit is a complex network of interrelationships. These relationships—and the total family system—contribute to who each person is. For example, if Dad had a bad day at the office, chances are that his arrival home and subsequent disposition will affect how he relates to members of his family and how they relate to him. Another example is divorce, which is essentially between the husband and wife. But their children as well as relatives and friends are significantly affected.

What does this mean to family ministry? A church leader needs to be thinking about how various programs of church ministry affect the entire family unit, not just one person. This principle has implications far beyond the present subject. You may be the only person in your family involved in church leadership. But your family is affected by your view of what that role entails.

Two observations can be made: First, it doesn't make sense to design programs that involve individuals, but totally ignore the environment and family system that produced them. For example, a program of Christian values and morality taught to young people needs to consider the home environment of the students. The teacher needs to determine to what degree the teaching will be supported by word and behavior in the family environment.

The second observation grows out of the first. It is wise to plan family activities that consider or include the family as a unit. Perhaps some activities could involve all family members, such as family retreats or parent-child Bible classes.

Application Activities

1. All systems—including the family, constantly interact with their environments. Interactions can be thought of as *exchanges.* Every biological organism can be viewed as a system. For example, people take in food and energy from the environment and give off wastes. A university is also a system. It requires many highly educated people and a lot of money—both of which are taken from society; but universities produce knowledge that is useful to society. Likewise, the family gives to and takes from both church and community—the larger environments of the family.

What needs do *families have?* Which of these needs are met by the church? Are some of these needs also met by the broader community? (Try to think of some specific needs of family groups.)

Families have much to give. They give in ways different from individuals. (For example, an individual can offer friendship, but a family can offer a sense of belonging.) How do families enrich a church? What do strong families give to a community?

Partners: the Home and Church

7 ***Family ministry should be home-centered, as well as church-centered.***

A debate has been going on for some time among Christian educators over the relationship between the home and church in the training of children. Is the church to take the lead in training children or is its primary role to equip *parents* to train their own children? What if parents do not fulfill this responsibility?

Most church leaders agree that in Christian families the home should take increasing responsibility for the nurturing of children. The church should be a supplement to parental efforts, not a substitute.

Church life is more distinct from family life than it should be. The biblical order of things is that church life should be patterned after the home life, rather than the reverse. The church family is an extension of several individual families or parts of families. The family analogy of God as father, Christ as the elder brother, the church as the bride, Christians as brothers and sisters, permeates the New Testament. The church and the home can have a mutually beneficial relationship, whereby both are strengthened. The possibility that the modern family will be underresponsible in the nurture of its children and that they will view the church as being overresponsible is a real one. Our next chapter will deal with how Christian nurture in the home can be effectively accomplished.

Application Activities

1. In light of the remarks about the home's and church's responsibilities for nurturing children, what responsibilities do you think belong primarily in the home? Which belong primarily in the church?

Beyond Words to Deeds

8 Family ministry needs to be experiential as well as factual.

In our society, learning facts is the normal way to obtain an education. In many areas of life, information is all that is needed. Providing information alone, however, is not a way to bring about changes in behavior or relationships. This statement is particularly true concerning marriage and family education. In churches where biblical authority is strongly emphasized, there is a tendency to view the teaching responsibilities on family life as simply getting the information out to the people.

The problem of how to bring about change is further complicated when it involves change in a relationship. Two or more people have to move together through a situation from discussion to insight to action. The problem and desired change need to be talked about in an objective and nonjudgmental manner. After exploring several alternatives, one is mutually chosen as the best. The new behavior must then take precedence.

In designing a learning experience for families, the Christian leader must keep in mind that the material will have to be experienced in a practical way if real learning and change is to take place.

In summary, learning can best be accomplished by implementing three simple steps: (1) tell the learners the information you want them to know; (2) show them (if necessary) how to apply the information; and (3) have them experience their own application of the information to their lives.

Application Activities

1. A famous educator once said, "If telling were teaching, we'd all be so smart we couldn't stand it." In other words, people don't remember everything they're told, nor do they put it into practice in their lives. Information and facts are needed, but more is needed if people are to *experience* better family life.

The following list contains several goals for various family ministry programs. Each one requires that people learn new information. But what do church leaders need to do to get people to *apply* the information and make the needed changes?

Goal: to promote family-centered worship in the home.

Information needed: What is worship? How families can worship together, resource materials

What more is needed?

Goal: to help parents take greater responsibility for educating their children about sex.

Information needed: information on what is being taught in the schools and how is it taught, an understanding of how children learn about sex and when, materials on the biblical view of sex.

What more is needed?

Goal: to reach out to older people in the community.

Information needed: needs of older people, how to relate to older people, names/addresses of senior citizens.

What more is needed?

Goal: to strengthen the church's support for divorced people.

Information needed: biblical view of divorce and marriage.

What more is needed?

Reaching Out to Families

9 Family ministry should be expanded to include the community.

The usual boundaries for developing a family life ministry lie within the context of the church fellowship. The model being proposed assumes a dual approach, with one emphasis on church families and the other on families in the community. This approach is based on the assumption that most people are interested in improving family and interpersonal relationships, and they will respond positively when they see their needs being met.

A word of warning. If these programs become "fronts" for high-pressure evangelism, community people will not get involved. Dealing with the spiritual dimensions of life is a legitimate concern for the church and one in which the church should be involved. But the *manner* in which it is presented is important. Community people should be able to hear various subjects presented from a Christian perspective without feeling pressured to conform to a particular set of beliefs. Spiritual concepts should be presented as a matter of choice rather than as a mandate. The church should strive to present its family material from a Christian viewpoint without needlessly offending people who do not share similar beliefs.

Application Activities

1. Following is a list of services that some churches have offered to members of the community—both Christian and non-Christian. In the two columns at the right, answer the following questions as they relate to each service.

1. Has your church ever offered this or a similar program? If so, what was the response from people outside your church fellowship?

2. Do you think your church could offer such a program, run it in a way that would not offend non-Christians, yet still be Christian? What problems might arise in trying to do this?

Program	*1*	*2*
Preschool or Day-care Center		
Youth Group Activities		
Recreational Sports		
Hot Meals to the Elderly		
Vacation Bible School		
Shut-in Visitation Service		

	1	2
food pantry		
tutoring services		
job placement counseling		
meals to parents of newborns		
divorce and marital counseling		
child abuse hotline		
food baskets to needy families		

Knowing What You Believe

10 Family ministry should operate from a theological foundation.

Theology should be an integral part of all that the church is and does. Each church should work out its own theological base for family ministry. What a church decides will determine the content and direction of the ministries.

The idea of a church working out its own "theology" may sound threatening. Yet it need not be. The task is simply to decide collectively what the Bible teaches about doctrines that will affect your ministry to families.

Following are some areas of concern that church leaders should address:

________________________ Nature, basis, and permanence of marriage (What does the Bible teach about the purpose of marriage, and under what conditions can the marriage vow be broken?)

________________________ Theology of divorce and remarriage (Will all divorced people be accepted into the fellowship? Will they be allowed to serve as church leaders? Who has a biblical justification for remarriage? Does conversion to Christ completely cleanse a person of past sins, or are there lasting implications for church life?)

________________________ Determination of legitimate lifestyles (What is to be done with singles who are known to be living with someone? What types of abnormal marital lifestyles are to be tolerated and what types are not?)

________________________ Nature and purpose of the family (What is the biblical view of family life?)

________________________ Theology of parenting (Is the Bible the infallible and eternal guide in parenting principles, or does it only reflect acceptable norms of parenting for its day? What styles of contemporary parenting are in accord with Christian principles and what are not?)

___________________________ Relationship between the family and the church (What part of training is the family itself to do and what part is the church to do?)

___________________________ Theology of sin, repentance, forgiveness, grace, and mercy as it relates to family matters (What do these doctrines teach in relation to how our families get along with one another?)

___________________________ Biblical authority as applied to these contemporary matters (How is the Bible to be interpreted—inerrant in all things, a guidebook, broad principles, eternal rules, or what?)

In raising all these issues, it should be noted that the inspiration and authority of God's Word is herein affirmed and believed by this author. However, the problem arises when good Christian people differ about what that infallible guide *says* on certain issues. My point is that an effective family ministry will uncover a multitude of problems that have theological implications. The wise church leader will anticipate as many of these problems as possible and try to obtain some type of workable consensus beforehand.

When practical or theological concerns arise in family matters, two things can happen, depending on how the problems are handled. If one or more church leaders take a position, set down policy, or announce a decision, the result will often be polarization, hard feelings, and mistrust. The person or people affected must either submit or leave. However, if leaders work with the particular individuals and family ministry leaders, they can learn from one another and apply God's Word in a loving manner. The process of working out a policy or theological basis for these issues shows everyone that the church truly cares about people, not just about enforcing its own standards. Helping others is a process that must begin with accepting people as they are—

then seeking God's best for each person and each family, using Scripture as our guide.

Application Activities

1. Review the "areas of concern" listed in the previous text. For which problem areas does your church already have policies?

In which problem areas has no foundation been laid? Has a lack of clarity on certain issues caused confusion or uncertainty in the church? If so, on which issues?

Getting It All Together

11 Family ministry needs to be integrated into every aspect of church life.

This statement focuses on the interrelatedness of family ministry with other existing functions of the church. Family ministry, as we have seen, is far more than adding activities or personnel. In fact, rather than building families up, additional activities may have the opposite effect—cause strain and fragmentation of families. Whatever we do must be integrated into the total life of the church.

One way integration can take place is for family programs to be developed within existing ministries. Two areas in particular lend themselves to this integration—the educational ministry, with various classes on Christian family life; and the youth ministry, with activities involving the whole family. Commitment to family *can* be and *should* be communicated through specific church programs.

Family ministry is also integrated with the entire ministry of the church through *attitudes* and *values.* A strong commitment to family on the part of key church leaders helps create a climate in which families bloom and prosper, and also a family-like atmosphere that permeates the entire church. It is harder to affect people's attitudes about the family than it is to provide services to families. But it is more important and long-lasting to change people's thinking and their values.

The integration of family ministry with the total church ministry—through programs and at the level of values—complement each other. As the church offers specific programs to serve families, people realize that the church (and its leaders) value the family. As church leaders give priority to the family, their decisions and actions will result in a ministry that serves families and also helps the church be and do all that God intends.

Application Activities

1. How would you describe a "climate in which families bloom and prosper," and "a family-like atmosphere that permeates the entire church"? What are the key differences between churches which have these characteristics and those that don't?

What can church leaders do to help create such a climate? (Be as specific as you can.)

Group Activities

Preparation for Group Meeting

Instructions for All Participants

Check off the following items as you prepare for the group meeting:

- ☐ *Read the chapter and complete the application activities.*
- ☐ *Look over the agenda for session 7.*
- ☐ *Write down your thoughts about the group task suggested under agenda item 3.*
- ☐ *Pray about concerns you've become aware of while preparing for this session.*

Leader's Instructions:

Preparation

- ☐ *Read the tips for session leaders (chapter 1).*
- ☐ *Read the chapter and the group activity agendas for sessions 6 and 7.*
- ☐ *Complete the exercises given in the chapter.*
- ☐ *Read all the leader's instructions (indicated in italics) before the meeting begins.*

Materials Needed

- ☐ *Newsprint, markers, masking tape, chalkboard, chalk.*

Group Meeting Agenda

1. Opening

- ☐ *If this study session is part of the regular meeting of a committee or class, check with the person in charge on the procedure for introducing this part of the meeting. Otherwise begin this session with prayer.*

Review of agenda (3–5 minutes)

- ☐ *Ask the group members how*

they felt about the last group session. Was there enough time? Was it a significant learning experience? Did the last meeting flow smoothly from one part to another?

☐ *If the group has a positive feeling about the last session they may choose to follow the agenda for session 6, with two changes:*

1 *In agenda item 2, the small group tasks are as follows:*

Group one: Promoting a family worship program.

Group two: Program to help parents deal with adolescent drug abuse.

2 *Instead of concentrating on the five foundational principles presented in chapter 6, group members should concentrate on the six principles found in chapter 7. (These are listed under agenda item 3.)*

☐ *If group members would like to try a different approach, they may use the following agenda. Otherwise, use the agenda for session 6.*

3. Large group activity (25–30 minutes)

Working as one group, members should develop a plan to implement a program to help parents deal with the problem of adolescent drug (and alcohol) abuse. The group (with the help of a recorder) should outline the basic steps it would take to plan a program, set objectives, identify participants, structure and schedule program activities, and get people involved.

In making plans, the group should try to remain consistent with as many of the foundational principles in this session as possible:

☐ *treating families as a system (a whole), rather than as individuals*

☐ *home-centered and church-centered*

☐ *experiential as well as informational*

☐ *includes services to community members*

☐ *operates from a theological foundation*

☐ *is integrated into the total church ministry*

☐ *Set a time limit and keep the group on schedule. It is important for the group to get down to business and list specific steps to take, rather than using the time to discuss all the alternatives and search for "the best" way. They will have a chance to analyze the plan in agenda items 4 and 5.*

☐ *The recorder may use a chalkboard or newsprint.*

4. Small group critique (10 minutes)

Members of each small group discuss the plan in the light of one or two of the six foundational principles presented in the chapter.

☐ *Form two, three, or six small groups, depending on the size of the large group. Each group should have at least two, but preferably three, members.*

☐ *Ask each group to take three, two, or one of the six principles (depending on the number of small groups).*

☐ *Each small group should have a reporter who will share with the large group under agenda item 5. If a small group is discussing more than one principle, it may have more than one reporter.*

5. Large group summary (20–25 minutes)

Reporters from each small group share with the large group either criticisms of the proposed program or suggestions for improving the program based on one of the six foundational principles.

- ☐ *As suggestions are shared, record them on the chalkboard or newsprint. Before going on to discuss another of the six principles, ask for discussion and recommendations for family ministry planners to use in planning other programs.*
- ☐ *After all reporters have shared about all six principles, ask if any other suggestions or principles should be included. Group members may want to reflect on all the principles they have learned in the last two sessions—discussing how they fit together or suggesting other principles that are needed.*

6. Closing and prayer

- ☐ *Ask for a group member to volunteer to lead the next group meeting.*
- ☐ *Close in prayer.*

NOTES

“In terms of the Great Commission, the implications for the Church are enormous. As a leader in the Church, it only makes sense that I ally myself with that primary group who can do the job of disciple-making most naturally and efficiently, that is, the family. To spend my time otherwise, just doesn't make sense.

But in reality, as leaders of the Church, we spend a great deal of our time trying to create new primary groups where there are none (such as in Sunday school classes, youth groups, small groups, etc.) while at the same time failing to nurture, stimulate and protect that primary group where the potential of disciple-making is going on every day and every night of the week. In truth, families make or break disciples, and in the process the task of the Church is made easier or more difficult.”

Dennis Guernsey, *A New Design for Family Ministry,* p. 11

Chapter 8
Family Enrichment in the Home

The Approach

We have seen that the Christian home plays a dominant role in the nurture of children. The nurture of adults in our families is equally important. If the home is the center for Christian training and growth, what should it be like?

In teaching about the Christian home we are tempted toward one of two extremes. We may paint such an idealistic picture that it becomes totally unrealistic and unattainable, thus producing guilt and discouragement. Or we play "isn't it awful" and only talk about what is wrong with family life, again producing discouragement.

In designing a ministry to families, we need to spend time thinking about the healthy Christian family life we want to promote. Recently, the trend in family life education has been toward the positive, "wellness model"—identifying and stressing family strengths rather than family faults. Positive examples inspire and are more effective in motivating people to change. We can isolate a number of traits usually found in strong families. Christian leaders will want to include these kinds of family patterns in their family ministry programs.

A Special Note

In the remainder of this chapter, you will be learning about seven positive traits that characterize strong families. As you look at each of these traits, read its description, and complete the application activities, you will be concerned about two things. First, you will be encouraged to look at each trait in the light of your own family life. Of course, the home is a very private place. It is impossible for an outsider or even an occasional visitor to know what is really going on inside someone else's home and family. The questions you answer about your own family life are intended to help you understand and apply the information you learn about each of the seven traits. If you are studying this book in a group setting, you will not be asked to share your answers with the others in your group, unless you choose to do so.

Every family can improve in all seven areas, and no one should feel embarrassed if they see a need for growth. One way to encourage growth might be to share this material with a spouse or other family members, to discuss the questions together, and to seek ways to work together for improvement in specific areas.

Our second concern in this session is to find ways that the leadership of the church can promote the health and well-being of its families. As church leaders, you are able to help others in the church strengthen their family life, particularly in these seven areas. Some of the application activities ask you to consider ways to do this, and most of the group session accompanying this chapter will be concerned with helping others.

One final note: these two areas of focus are related. If church leaders themselves have weak families, they may be hindered when attempting to help others in the church. People learn a great deal about family life by what they see in others. Do elders respect and honor their wives? Are leaders so involved in church activities that they have no time for their families? **Perhaps the greatest thing church leaders can do to help other families is to set a good example.** Without this, the entire family ministry of a church can be undermined.

Christian Family Strengths

1 Healthy communication patterns.

Communication is to the family what blood is to the body. Even strong families have squabbles and disagreements. But by working through issues they keep disagreements from becoming full-blown problems. The difference between families is not the presence or absence of conflict, but the way in which conflict is handled.

What elements make up healthy family communication? Read through the following list.

1 They are active listeners. The quality of listening is the most difficult element in the communication process.

2 They speak the truth in love. This virtue is one of the marks of a maturing person, according to Paul in Ephesians 4:15. Truth and love are essential as family members relate to one another.

3 They have mutual respect and consideration. Healthy families are unselfish, and their communication patterns reflect this.

4 They can freely express their feelings. Each family member can express his or her own emotions without being threatened.

5 Their individual differences are recognized and accepted. There's no pressure to conform—to all act and think alike.

6 They know how to negotiate skillfully

through conflicts. They have learned how to listen to another, to explore and define problem areas, to identify their contributions to those problems, to state their goals and to work toward resolutions.

All of these skills can be taught. Teaching these qualities of family communication is essential in building strong Christian families.

2 Affirmation, support, appreciation.

Another significant quality of strong families is that they continually express appreciation for each other. They build one another up and make others feel good about themselves. It's a universal human need—the need to be appreciated, especially by those we love most. A critical spirit within a family has far-reaching negative effects. Out of it flows all sorts of problems. Appreciation needs to be expressed if a relationship is to grow. This quality can also be taught.

Application Activities

Looking Homeward

1. God has given us several useful "checklists" for communication in the home (and elsewhere). How does your family measure up?

	Usually not a problem	Needs improvement
"Each of you must put off falsehood and speak truthfully to his neighbor" (Eph. 4:25).		
"Do not let any		

unwholesome talk come out of your mouths, but only what is helpful for building others up according to their needs, that it may benefit those who listen" (4:29).		
"Get rid of all bitterness, rage and anger, brawling and slander, along with every form of malice" (4:31)		
"Be kind and compassionate one to another, forgiving each other" (4:32).		
"Speak to one another with psalms, hymns, and spiritual songs" (5:19).		
"Always giving thanks to God the Father for everything" (5:20).		
"Everyone should be quick to listen, slow to speak, and slow to become angry" (James 1:19)		

2. What are some *specific ways* you can help affirm and build up others in your family? Write down a few ways those relationships can be found in your family.

____

Your Spouse

____

Your Child

____

Your Parents

____

Other Relatives

____

Which of these relationships needs the most work?

Helping Others

3. A Case Study. The following is part of a dialogue between Tim and Mary. Tim is a leader in the church. He has responsibility for the children's Bible School program. Mary is an active member of the church. She is a single parent whose daughter is involved in Bible school.

MARY: "Tim, may I speak to you for a minute?"

TIM: "Sure, go ahead. I'm on my way to lunch, but I can spare a few minutes."

MARY: "I was talking with a neighbor of mine the other day, Mrs. Ramsey. She and her husband don't come to church very often, but have been sending their two sons to Bible class. Recently, one of the boys got multiple sclerosis and is confined to a wheelchair. He is embarrassed to come anymore, and his brother feels awkward coming alone. Is there anything—"

TIM (interrupting): "Oh yes, I've talked to Mrs. Ramsey on the phone several times. Last time it was for over half an hour. I've explained to her that it would be difficult getting a wheelchair in here right now because we haven't built that ramp yet."

MARY: "What about the other brother? Surely if some of the other boys in the class befriended him—"

TIM: "I know what you're thinking, but you can't count on kids for that kind of commitment. It's a tough situation, I know, and I'm praying about it. Maybe something will come up. Let me know if you think of anything else. I'm sorry, I really have to go now."

MARY: "But—"

How do you think Mary feels at this point?

In what ways did Tim fail to communicate well with Mary?

How did he fail to affirm Mary for what she was trying to do?

What is Mary likely to think or feel about the church's ministry to families?

What will the Ramseys think?

What lessons can church leaders learn from this case study about helping other families?

4. Family life experts say that communication in the home should be 80 percent positive and 20 percent negative. Why do you think they say this? Do you agree or disagree? Explain your answer.

Commitment and Responsibility

3 Sense of trust, mutual respect, and shared responsibility.

In a strong Christian family, the husband and wife set the tone for all of these traits by demonstrating them in their own relationship. Trust has to be earned, but when it is broken, it can be mended. Mutual respect first involves self-respect, then respect for the individuality of others.

Parents also need to teach the relationship between responsibility and self-esteem to their children. Children are taught to be responsible, which should include living with the logical consequences of irresponsibility. Children who are consistently rescued from the consequences of their misbehavior and wrong choices are not prepared to live as independent, responsible adults.

4 Basic commitment to the family.

Commitment, like happiness, is a by-product of other qualities. Commitment is easy when certain elements are present in the family. We have already mentioned some of these—respect, trust, acceptance, affirmation. We could add unselfishness, shared responsibility, understanding, and honesty. A sense of tradition also keeps a family together. When these other elements are weakened or missing— such as during a family crisis—a basic loyalty or commitment to the family motivates members to restore family relationships.

This deep sense of kinship enables families to stand together during adversity—and to emerge stronger from a crisis. Other families may be fractured by such experiences, but families who have cultivated commitment grow closer to each other and to God through the process.

Unconditional love and sacrificial commitment to marriage and family are not popular themes in our culture. Nevertheless, they are needed, and wise church leaders will emphasize the nurturing of the family unit.

Application Activities

Looking Homeward

1. Trusting others in our families means we believe they will fulfill their responsibilities in life—to us and to others. Trust is not always mutual, simply because not everyone—including people in our own family—are equally trustworthy. Our own actions determine how trustworthy we are and how much trust others can place in us. When we fail to fulfill our responsibilities, we make it harder for others to trust us. The following list of actions undermine trust in a family or marriage. Have you or others in your family been consistently guilty of some of these? If so, is there anything you can do to restore trust—either by fulfilling your own responsibilities or helping others to do so?

Not keeping one's commitments

Lying about or denying one's own responsibilities

____

Gossiping (whereby a person shows he/she is not fulfilling responsibility to forgive and accept others)

____

Flirting (a form of lying about one's commitments)

____

Taking responsibility away from others (for example, by fulfilling others' commitments for them)

____

Using someone else's property or resources for purposes other than which they were intended (A good "trustee," by contrast, is one who can be trusted to take proper care of another's property.)

____

Can you add to this list other actions which undermine trust?

2. Mutual respect and shared responsibility are signs of healthy families. In practical terms, mutual respect means that individuals within the family know one another, appreciate the worth of each other, and respect the rights that others have to be themselves. Measuring these things is difficult, but perhaps you can use the following exercise to help you or others in your family increase your appreciation and respect for one another:

Choose one person in your family. On a piece of paper, make a list of everything you think this person has done today, starting with the time he or she got up this morning. Then go to that person and ask them what they have done today.

(Often we don't realize how much others—especially those closest to us—do that directly contribute to family relationships.)

Once you have done this with one or more people in your family, take time to thank God for the others in your family. Pray that you will grow in respect for one another.

Helping Others

3. Most church programs are flexible enough to focus—in one way or another—on family life. In a prayer meeting, one can pray for family members. In times of fellowship, one can focus on enjoying fellowship in Christ with family members. Families can worship together and even do evangelism together.

Select a church program, preferably one in which you hold a leadership role.

Design an activity that (1) fits in with the format of your program, and (2) promotes mutual respect, shared responsibility, or loyalty among family members. Some of the following questions may help you plan such an activity:

What outcomes would you like the activity to have? (What should people do differently after the activity?)

What is the nature of the activity?
Learning (helping others know something about better family life)

Celebrating (helping others appreciate the family life they have)

Doing (helping others do something about their family life)

How will you explain the purpose of the activity?

Will people need any materials to perform the activity?

What preparation would you need to do?

Is there any way to follow up on the activity, or will it be a one-time experience?

Do you need permission from other church leaders (or from the group of people themselves) to conduct the activity?

Will the activity help people assume greater responsibility for the health of their own families? How?

Time for Family and Others

5 Spend time together.

It's hard to express appreciation or communicate without being together. Experts agree that the lack of time spent together may be the biggest single enemy of today's family. Church leaders, seeking to strengthen Christian family life, might focus on this area from a number of different perspectives.

We are not promoting a "smothering" type of togetherness, where individuality is damaged. We are discussing the fragmenting effect our hectic pace of life has on family togetherness. It's hard to have *quality* time without spending some *quantity* of time together.

If parents are to teach their children the way of the Lord, they have to spend time with them. Church leaders have a tough challenge—to come up with creative and workable ways for families to spend quality time together. To get you started, consider the following:

1 Be aware of your level of involvement in organized activities, especially involving the children.

2 Control your work schedule.

3 Develop a family "philosophy" of leisure and together time, allowing for individual differences.

4 Have regularly scheduled family times.

5 Don't do everything together, but do *something* together.

The best place to start working on family together times is with your own.

*6 **Religious convictions and values.***

We can only pass our Christian faith on to our children if they see its direct benefit in improving the quality of our lives together. Does Christianity work? Does God really make a difference in our daily lives? These questions demand honest answers. Strong Christian families answer these questions with an enthusiastic yes. These Christian qualities can be incorporated into family ministry and show the value of deep religious commitment. One fruit of Christianity is a shared sense of purpose and meaning in life. This results in a clearly defined spiritual lifestyle found in every dimension of a family's relationship. A godly lifestyle enables us to draw strength and support from God and each other. The Christian virtues of patience, forgiveness, handling of anger, and maintaining a positive attitude are made easier and more functional in a family that is united in a spiritual commitment.

Strong Christian parents are not afraid to live out their values in front of their children—thereby teaching them what is right, wrong, and important in life.

*7 **Reach out to others.***

In our attempt to improve the quality of family life, it would be a big mistake to leave out this element. Strong Christian families value service to others. They do not exist simply for their own satisfaction. They maintain a primary focus inward, but realize the good that can be done by reaching out to the lives of other people. Generally speaking, families who care about others have simpler lifestyles and do not have an overabundance of this world's goods. They have something far more valuable. They have discovered what Jesus taught—that true happiness and fulfillment come from a self-giving, self-emptying life.

We can take this profound theological concept and filter it down to our churches and even to our own homes.

Application Activities

Looking Homeward

1. List all the activities that your entire family has been involved in together during the past week.

What quantity of time did each activity involve?

How do you feel about the "quality" of time spent on each activity?

Is there a key difference or attitude that distinguishes "quality time" from "quantity time"? What is it?

2. Our religion must be *lived* if we expect it to become a living faith for our children. Forget about all you have told your children about God or His Word; pretend they have never heard or read about Jesus or the Gospel. What would they see *in your life* that would point them to faith in God?

3. Is your family involved in any form of outreach? In what ways is your family—as a family—of service to others in the church or community?

Helping Others

4. Consider how the families in your church spend their time. What percentage of their time is spent . . .

	% Spent	% Should Spend
away from each other and away from church?		
together at home?		
together at church?		
at church but separated?		

In the right-hand column give percentages for the way you think families ought to spend their time. (Make sure the total in each column is 100 percent.)

What can church leaders do to encourage families to spend more time together at home?

at church?

5. List any ways that you can think of for families—working together as a family—to be of service to others.

Apart from being an example, how can church leaders encourage families to be involved in such activities?

Group Activities

Preparation for Group Meeting

Instructions for All Participants

Check off the following items as you prepare for the group meeting:

- ☐ Read the chapter and complete the application activities.
- ☐ Look over the agenda for session 8.
- ☐ Make a note of any questions or comments you have about what you have read for this session or the application activities you have completed (discuss them under agenda item 4).
- ☐ Write down your thoughts or reactions to the discussion questions suggested under agenda item 4.
- ☐ Pray about concerns you've become aware of while preparing for this session.

Leader's Instructions:

Preparation

- ☐ *Read the tips for session leaders (chapter 1).*
- ☐ *Read the chapter and the group activity agenda for session 8.*

- ☐ *Complete the exercises given in the chapter.*
- ☐ *Read all the leader's instructions (indicated in italics) before the meeting begins.*

Materials Needed

- ☐ *Newsprint, markers, masking tape, chalkboard, chalk.*

Group Meeting Agenda

1. Opening

- ☐ *If this study session is part of the regular meeting of a committee or class, check with the person in charge on the procedure for introducing this part of the meeting. Otherwise begin this session with prayer.*

2. Large group activity (10–15 minutes) Review of case study (application activity 3)

- ☐ *Ask two group members to take the parts of Tim and Mary and read through the case study (Application Activity 3).*
- ☐ *Ask people to share with the group the answers they wrote to the questions following the dialogue.*
- ☐ *As the members share their answers to the last question, summarize key ideas on the chalkboard or newsprint. Leave the list on display throughout the session.*

3. Small group prayer (optional, 5–10 minutes)

Church leaders do not need perfect family lives in order to be good examples, but they should be actively seeking practical ways to love their families more. If group members feel a need for support from others in doing this, they may find a short time of prayer with others helpful.

- ☐ *Form several small groups of two, three, or four people.*
- ☐ *Suggest that each small group member share one area that they feel a need for improvement in their family life before the group goes to prayer.*

4. Large group discussion (25–30 minutes)

- ☐ *Ask the group which of the following topics they would like to discuss.*
- ☐ *In addition, at this time individuals may bring up questions or comments they had about the chapter for consideration by the entire group.*

Discussion topics:

1 A family life expert once remarked that families in a particular church might be better off if the church canceled half its programs and cut its paid staff down to half time. Why do you think he made such a statement? Does the statement have any validity?

2 Training Christian children is a task that belongs to both the family and the church, though God places primary responsibility on the family. What is the church's responsibility in training children? Should the church fulfill these responsibilities by working directly with children, or indirectly with children, or indirectly through parents, or both? Can the church ever take too much responsibility?

3 Suppose that for one week, any time any adult member of the church performed a duty (such as leading a Bible School class or visiting a person in need), he or she was required to do it with one or more other family members.

What might happen (both good and bad results)? Are there some situations in which this wouldn't work (where it is either impossible or inappropriate)? Why wouldn't it work in those situations?

5. Small group activity (10–15 minutes)

Working in small groups, members should write on newsprint, principles or suggestions to help church leaders in strengthening families.

- ☐ *Divide members into groups of three or four.*
- ☐ *Encourage members to work quickly, using what they have read and learned in the group session. The small groups should put their ideas down on paper in sentences or phrases others would understand.*
- ☐ *After all groups have listed four or five ideas, have them post the newsprint sheets. Members should spend a few minutes reading the ideas generated by other groups.*
- ☐ *After the session is over, collect the sheets and save them for use by other church leaders interested in family ministry.*

6. Closing and prayer

- ☐ *Remind the person who is tabulating the responses to the congregational survey and/or community survey to tabulate the responses and bring a copy for each group member to the next session.*
- ☐ *Ask for a group member to volunteer to lead the next group member.*
- ☐ *Close in prayer.*

NOTES

"A desperate situation often occasions short-term solutions that fail and lead to sullen resignation. . . . And in contemporary family life, complex issues require long-range solutions, not simple answers and faddish programs. Remedies will have to be based on an in-depth analysis of the family, just as effective treatment follows careful diagnosis."

Charles Sell, *Family Ministry*,
p. 33.

Chapter 9
Vital Questions to Ask

A Different Approach

The method church leaders use to implement various family ministries often makes the difference between success and failure of the overall program. A series of questions must be dealt with if family life outreach is to become a reality. Failure to address the issues raised will result in poor execution of what might have been an excellent program.

In this chapter, instead of having two or three "application activities" you will be asked to write your response to each question. Answer the questions as they relate to your own church.

Vital Questions

1. *Does the congregation see a need for improved family life?*

There is a vast difference in potential between a few vocal members in favor of a family emphasis and widespread interest and support of such a program. What is the opinion of the average member? Where there is no perceived need, there is no support—financial, or otherwise.

If the need is not sufficiently seen, the first step may be an "awareness" campaign to emphasize not only local and church family needs, but the potential a family ministry can offer. Use some of the material covered in previous sessions, and as much local evidence as you can find, to establish a real need.

How much of a need does your congregation see?

2. *Is the congregation prepared to do something about it?*

Being aware of the need for a family ministry program is not enough. It should be determined whether or not the church is prepared to implement such a program. The questionnaire that can be administered to the members may help gauge this readiness.

Other indications of readiness are:

Personal experiences of breakdowns in family life.

Burden for relevant forms of community outreach.

Willingness to commit people and resources to family problems.

Dissatisfaction with current ministries to families.

What is your opinion of the congregation's readiness?

3. *What is the commitment of various leaders toward improving the quality of family life in the church and community? What is your relationship to these leaders?*

Three levels of leadership need particular attention. Variations of these levels depend on the particular church's organizational structure. The central figure in determining the success or failure of a family ministry is the person who occupies the pulpit. He is the congregation's major opinion-setter. The minister's public endorsements are vital, and his silence on matters (not to mention his opposition) can be fatal.

Another level of leadership whose commitment needs to be assessed is the body of local leaders, such as elders, deacons, or a key committee. Their support is also vital, so they should be involved in the early stages of planning.

The third level of leadership involvement is the church staff—where there are multiple-staff situations. These leaders need to see the integrative nature of family ministry and how their individual ministries can benefit.

The second part of the question asks about your relationships to these leaders. It may be that members of your group come from the second level of leadership—elders and deacons. The pulpit minister or other staff members may be studying the materials with you. But it's also possible that many of your group do not currently hold such leadership positions in your church. In that case, you must consider where your group stands in relation to the recognized leaders of the church. Do the church leaders recognize and support the members of your group? (If not, you may have a long, uphill struggle to gain credibility.) How much influence do members of your group have over leadership opinions? Are there others in the church who have more influence than your group? Can these people be asked to help sway the opinions of other church leaders and the congregation as a whole?

What do you think are the opinions of various church leaders toward family ministry?

____
Pulpit minister

____
Elders and Deacons

____
Other Staff (if applicable)

What kind of credibility does your group have in the eyes of each of these types of leaders?

____
Pulpit Minister

____
Elders and Deacons

____
Other staff

4. *What type of family ministry is anticipated?*

Several factors must be considered to answer this question. The program model introduced in chapter 6 will be helpful here. What you do (classes for church families, community courses, support groups, library, counseling) depends on the talent and resources available.

Your philosophy also affects the direction of family ministry. Every church has its own unique approach to ministry—the patterns and priorities of one congregation are different from those of other congregations. The approach to family ministry in your church must be shaped by your church's philosophy and style of ministry.

For example, every church has its own approach to evangelism. We have already seen that effective family ministry needs to have a dual commitment—to the members and nonmembers. *How* a church goes about reaching out to non-Christian families is crucial.

If community people and other church people discover that family programs are only a thinly-veiled front for high-pressure evangelism, the public aspect of the program is doomed. A better approach is to deal first with the immediate needs of people and at an appropriate time, with their permission, deal with the spiritual implications of where they are.

Of course, everything doesn't have to begin at once. Start with programs that have a good chance for success. Consult your church survey for areas of high interest.

What types of family ministry do you anticipate for your church? What are key programs or services that your church should provide for families?

5. *Who is the ministry designed to reach?*

There are two basic approaches that need to be discussed. The first is to design a ministry aimed primarily at church families. The second is to include the community people as well.

A combined approach is the most desirable. A combination of church and community family enrichment is ideal. The purpose of the church is to serve people and meet their deeper needs. Nonmembers tend to be more responsive to the spiritual dimension of their lives when the church gives them assistance with their family relational needs. An effective family outreach says to a community that the church is interested in people and what happens to them.

In planning family ministry it may be helpful to identify—both within and outside the church—the people you are trying to reach. Not all groups of people will be equally served by a church's family ministry, simply because people have different needs and some of those needs are more important than others. Different types of programs—whether prevention, enrichment, or counseling—should be structured to meet the needs of specific family groups. For example, your community may have a special need for a program that offers counseling and assistance to unwed mothers. Or your church may have a special need for a program that is preventive in nature and seeks to help parents of adolescents be better parents. In terms of enrichment programs, it is difficult to target specific family types—all families need this type of positive emphasis.

When identifying community members who will benefit from a family outreach program, the size of your city is a determining factor. The approach of a church in a small town and one in a large city would be different, for instance, in the type and method of advertising chosen. Other things to consider are the type of people living within the area and the location of the church facilities.

In planning to minister to families both in the church and the community, target groups need to be identified. Everyone should be welcomed, but each church will have areas of strength and interests that will particularly appeal to certain individuals. The problem is complex and needs the attention of church leaders.

What family types should your church be trying to reach with the following types of programs?

	In the church	In the community
Prevention		
Enrichment		
Counseling		

(Note: At some future point, church leaders may find it helpful to repeat this exercise for family programs of differing priorities. For example, who is our primary target for preventive programs in the church? Who is our secondary target? etc.)

6. *What similar services are available through community organizations and other churches?*

Planners need to be aware of the types of offerings that are available elsewhere. In some cases, duplication is needless and should be avoided. Other services, because of the widespread need for them, could legitimately be duplicated, such as divorce support groups, widows' groups, parenting and marriage enrichment courses, etc. Some services may need to be duplicated because other agencies do not have a biblical basis and this approach is essential to the health of families in your church.

In certain situations, a church might be unable to offer a particular program by itself but could do so on a cooperative basis with other churches. Examples of cooperative efforts include: (1) counseling services, (2) film series and speakers, and (3) course offerings.

Cooperative efforts are generally more cost effective than individual ones. By working together, churches will be able to make a greater impact on community family life than any one church can alone.

What is your assessment of programs already available in your community? How can you cooperate?

7. *What human and material resources will be needed to implement a family ministry in your church?*

The availability and willingness of volunteers is essential for an effective ministry to families. They are needed for planning, implementing, and evaluating programs. Involvement in these aspects of family ministry becomes a unique growth experience for each volunteer who participates. Everyone in a church is a potential volunteer since everyone has had experience as a family member. Church members who do volunteer become the lifeblood of the church—making family ministry a reality.

Christians have an excellent opportunity to be involved in all levels of service. They can participate as lay counselors ("peoplehelpers), helpers with special activities, teachers, typists, bookkeepers, librarians, promotional consultants, and in any other activities where they can use their talents of vocation and service.

Family ministry planners will want to consider the contributions the existing staff could make to the overall program. In most churches, family ministries will be led by existing staff people and other church leaders and will not involve the hiring of a family or counseling specialist. A spirit of cooperation and involvement at the staff level prevents a self-contained program and allows the staff to develop and integrate family ministry with their other areas of responsibility. One key to staff cooperation and enthusiastic support is to involve them in the early planning stages and let them pick areas of involvement they feel comfortable with.

For larger churches, involvement in family ministry might mean hiring additional personnel. The size of the ministry and the availability of resources will determine if more staff is needed. Whoever heads the ministry should try to match individual strengths to particular program needs. For instance, if you design a highly visible community-oriented program, you will want to find someone with good organizational, social, and speaking skills, as well as family relationship expertise. If your ministry is primarily a counseling service, that job description will call for a different set of skills.

Another question that needs to be addressed concerns building facilities. Can you use present church facilities? Or will additional facilities need to be built, purchased, or rented? Flexibility is essential. Start with what you have. Don't let facilities keep you from beginning some form of family outreach.

How do you think your church will use volunteers? Will it use existing staff? Will it need to hire additional staff? Is there a need for additional facilities?

8. *What kinds of media are available to publicize the church's ministry?*

Promotion is an essential ingredient in an effective family outreach. A church may have one of the finest programs available anywhere, but if the public doesn't know about it, the program cannot strengthen families. The degree of media influence varies from city to city, with television, newspapers, and radio competing for prominence. Conversations with established community leaders and rating reports will reveal the media with the greatest influence or largest audience.

In addition to media coverage, the most valuable publicity tool you could have are your own people who are enthusiastic about the family ministry program. They can help you tremendously through public speaking engagements and private conversations.

What is your opinion about how effective you can be in spreading the word about this ministry to families in your community?

How can you promote the family ministry within your own church?

9. *How will families be involved in planning, running, and improving your church's family ministry?*

A family ministry program doesn't exist for its own sake. Having a lot of family-oriented activities printed in your Sunday bulletin may look good, but it doesn't automatically make your church a better church. And, while we want people to come to our churches, family life programs can't be used as bait to get people in the door. Family programs exist to *serve families*—both in the church and in the community. If church leaders do all the planning and running of family programs, there is no guarantee that the programs will actually *help* families. The families we serve have a very important stake in our programs of service and must have a meaningful part in helping plan and run those programs.

We are talking about ownership here. People tend to value programs in which they have an active part. They tend to participate in programs that meet their real needs—not the needs that someone else may think they have. How do people come to "own" a family life program? By taking at least some of the responsibility for planning, running, and improving the program.

Of course, church leaders may need to provide coordination, direction, and, in some cases, resources. But ultimately it is people who help people—not information, money, or good intentions. So people—families—need to be involved in deciding what they need. Families need to be involved in ministering to others. Families need to be involved in making programs of service more effective and relevant.

The participation of families in all aspects of a family ministry does more than just keep the programs going. The act of being involved in activities that benefit others also benefits those who help carry out those activities. By helping others, people help themselves. When family members or families take on responsibility for ministering to other families, they have a unique opportunity for personal growth and family development.

Involving people in family ministry is a vital concern for church leaders. Paid staff, recognized church leaders, and trained professionals cannot hope to meet all the needs of families in churches and communities today. People themselves—families—must be involved.

How can you help the families in your church and community to be meaningfully involved in planning programs to benefit them?

In running those programs?

In improving those programs?

Group Activities

Preparation for Group Meeting

Instructions for All Participants

Check off the following items as you prepare for the group meeting:

- ☐ Read the chapter and complete the application activities.
- ☐ Look over the agenda for session 9.
- ☐ Make a note of any questions or comments you have about what you have read for this session (discuss them under agenda item 4).
- ☐ Write down your thoughts or reactions to the discussion questions suggested under agenda item 4.
- ☐ Pray about concerns you've become aware of through your preparation for this session.

Leader's Instructions:

Preparation

- ☐ *Read the tips for session leaders (chapter 1).*
- ☐ *Read the chapter and the group activity agenda for session 9.*
- ☐ *Complete the exercises given in the chapter.*
- ☐ *Read all the leader's instructions (indicated in italics) before the meeting begins.*

Materials Needed

- ☐ *Newsprint, markers, masking tape, chalkboard, chalk.*

Group Meeting Agenda

1. Opening

☐ *If this study session is part of the regular meeting of a committee or class, check with the person in charge on the procedure for introducing this part of the meeting. Otherwise begin this session with prayer.*

2. Small group activity (15–20 minutes)

Each small group will consider three of the nine "vital questions for family ministry" raised in the chapter. Group members should share what each wrote in answer to the questions, discuss any difference of opinion, and try to come to a group consensus.

☐ *Divide the group into three smaller groups of approximately equal size. Assign questions 1, 4, and 7 to one group, 2, 5, and 8 to another group, and 3, 6, and 9 to the third group.*

☐ *Each small group should appoint a recorder and reporter. Have the recorder write down on newsprint or a chalkboard key words reflecting the group's thinking on each question.*

☐ *If, after several minutes, small group members cannot reach a consensus on one of the questions, they should record their differing opinions, and go on to another question. After discussing all three questions, they may go back to discuss a previous question if time permits.*

3. Large group activity (25–30 minutes)

Each small group reports to the large group its answers to the three assigned questions. Other group members are free to respond, ask for clarification, or state differing opinions.

Group members may wish to use the space provided on page 159 to respond to the following nine questions in the "NOTES":

1. Does the congregation see a need for improved family life?
2. Is the congregation prepared to do something about it?
3. What is the commitment of various leaders toward improving the quality of family life in the church and community, and what is your relationship to those leaders?
4. What type of family ministry do you anticipate for your church? What are key programs or services that your church should provide for families?
5. What family types (in the church and in the community) should your church be trying to reach with preventive programs? With enrichment programs? With counseling programs?
6. What similar services are available through community organizations and other churches?
7. Do you think your church will (a) use volunteers? (b) use existing staff? (c) need additional staff? (d) need additional facilities?
8. How effective can your church be in letting the community know about your church's ministry to families? How can you promote the family ministry in your own church?
9. How can you help families in your church and community get involved in planning, running, and improving family programs intended to benefit them?

☐ *Answer each of the above questions in numerical order. Encourage the small group reporters to move along, so you average three minutes on each question. When the group as a whole is in general agreement go to the next question. When there is wide disagreement, the group should note the differing opinions and move on. (Additional time for discussion may be available under agenda item 4.)*

- ☐ *You may want to keep a written record of the answers given by the small groups so they can be typed, duplicated, and distributed the following week. You may want to ask one person to volunteer to write down the ideas as they are shared, or ask each small group's recorder to give you his notes after the meeting.*

4. Large group discussion (10–15 minutes)

Major topic for discussion:

1 About which of the nine questions was there the most disagreement? Why did people disagree? Is there any special action the group should take as a result of this disagreement?

- ☐ *At this time, members may bring up questions or comments they had about the chapter.*

5. Closing and prayer

- ☐ *Pass out the results of the congregational and/or community survey to all group members to use in preparing for session 10.*
- ☐ *Ask for a group member to volunteer to lead the next group meeting.*
- ☐ *Close in prayer.*

NOTES

“If the church is built around its institutional and numerical growth, demanding from its members so much time and energy that home life suffers, it will broadcast a negative message about the home that no Mother’s Day sermon can overcome. Expressing family-life ministry in this larger context will require the following: selecting church leaders who hold that the family is to be in a position of priority and who relate in a Christlike manner in both the home and the church; planning the budget with expressions of Christian values in mind; planning the program of the church so it does not compete with the family but rather involves it in church life; developing the church’s evangelistic thrust so that whole families are reached, not split up; providing services and fellowship for singles, divorced, widowed, single parents, and others who need the church as ‘family’; recognizing the family unit in announcements and printed messages; building the church’s Christian-education program so that it is integrated with the home instead of being a separate program, sufficient in itself. . . .”

Charles Sell, *Family Ministry,*
p. 87

Chapter 10
Planning For Family Ministry: Getting Started

Laying a firm foundation for family ministry is important. Sooner or later, however, you have to build something on that foundation. In building a family ministry, you don't have to build a whole "house" at once. But you should plan far enough in advance so that the different parts of the house go well together.

The material in previous chapters of *Ministering to Families* has provided a broad and solid foundation on which to build a family ministry. Beginning with chapters 3 and 4 on contemporary family needs and needs assessment, you have been considering the needs of families in your church and community. No doubt you have already gained many insights about how your church's family ministry can help families. You have an idea of what functions you want your "house," or family ministry, to serve. But how do you translate those ideas into "blueprints" or plans for your family ministry? How do you begin building the program? How do you get the church to "buy" the plan and to take ownership of the house as it is being built? These questions and others will be addressed in this final chapter. You will begin to plan your family life ministry.

Questionnaire Results

If your committee chose to use the family ministry questionnaire or neighborhood interview methods of needs assessment, you are in a better position to plan for the needs of families in your church and community than if you had not used these methods. But what should you do with all the information you have obtained? What does all the information obtained tell you about family needs in your church? And what should you do about those needs?

The sample family ministry questionnaire in appendix A asks for several types of information. First, it asks for personal data about the individual respondent and his or her family. This type of information will help family ministry planners construct a family profile of the congregation. It can answer such questions as: How many families have children in a given age-group? What proportion of respondents are single parents? divorced? widowed? never married? What proportion of respondents are in a given age-group? From this type of information, family ministry planners can gain a more accurate picture of the people they are trying to serve. Family life committee members may be surprised to find that some of the data runs contrary to their assumptions about the congregation.

Another type of question found on the family ministry questionnaire will yield information on the respondent's feelings and opinions about his or her family life. These questions will help family ministry planners determine how open the congregation is to change and what types of family ministry programs would be most welcome. If most people feel they have strong families, are satisfied with their marriages, and have regular family-oriented activities, there will probably be less need for family enrichment programs. If this is the case, the family life committee may want to focus on the few people who are dissatisfied with their family relationships and seek to provide preventive and/or counseling services to meet their needs.

Several questions yield information on respondents' attitudes toward current church programs (or the lack thereof). The question dealing with the place of singles can indicate the need for programs which demonstrate a commitment to these people. The open-ended question asking how the church can help increase the quality of family life (item #6) should be seriously considered by the committee. A question of this type represents important felt needs of the congregation.

Perhaps the heart of the questionnaire are the two long items (#19 and #22) which give respondents opportunity to express their interest in or need for particular types of family ministry. Since these questions ask for the most specific type of information on the questionnaire, they will be valuable in planning specific types of service. The relative numbers of people expressing interest in similar items also helps planners prioritize which types of needs are most widely felt by the congregation.

The questions corresponding to the two long items but which ask about the ability to help *provide* specific services (#20 and #23) yield information useful for a different purpose. From these, the family life committee can get an idea how easy a particular program will be to initiate and operate, and ultimately, how successful the program will likely be. For example, if 75 percent of the respondents feel there is a need for a ministry to older adults, but only 5 percent are willing to be involved, this may be a ministry which currently lacks adequate support. The committee should seek other ways to generate commitment to meet this need before it undertakes such a ministry.

Finally, questions about church participation patterns and schedule preferences can help in programming family ministry.

All of these types of information can be obtained by tabulating the questionnaire data supplied by the respondents. More information can be obtained when correlation techniques are used. That is, it is possible to compare how many individual respondents answered *two or more questions* in the same way. For example, how many of the people who said they work more than 60 hours a week outside the home (item #30) *also* said they were dissatisfied with their marriage (#11) and do things with their family infrequently (item #16)?

If you have people in your church who are skilled in analyzing such relationships, you may want them to answer particular questions the committee has about such correlations. (It is not possible to explain here how this can be done.) To obtain meaningful results from such analysis, you should have a large number of respondents. To do this type of analysis, it is also necessary to have all the actual questionnaires, not just the tabulations of responses to each item. For most churches, an analysis of information from the tabulations of individual questionnaire items will be more than adequate.

Neighborhood Interview Result

The neighborhood interview (appendix C) is a different method of needs analysis on a different group of people—families in the community. If your committee chose to conduct neighborhood interviews, you are in a better position to understand the needs of families in your community. However, in comparing the results of the neighborhood interviews with the congregational questionnaires, the interviews will give you a less complete view of community needs than the questionnaire gave you of congregational needs. Nonetheless, the interviews give useful information. In addition, the process of conducting the interviews has helped the members of your committee gain a better "feel" for the family needs in your community.

The types of information gathered from neighborhood interviews will likely be more limited than those gleaned from the congregational questionnaire. For example, interviews do not give a reliable family profile for your community. That is, you will not have an accurate picture of what family patterns (single parents, divorced people, elderly living alone, never married, etc.) exist in your community and what the prevalence of each pattern is. (This type of information is probably more readily obtainable from sources such as the census bureau or department of social services.)

Respondents are not asked their opinions about the quality of their own family life, since they are not likely to give an unfavorable response to someone they just met. Nor are they asked their opinions about current church programs, since they are probably not familiar with them.

The greatest value of neighborhood interviews is the information on the *interests in family services* expressed in response to the long lists of possible church programs listed on the Neighborhood Interview Inventories in appendix C. The responses to these two items should be treated equally, since some people will project their own needs and interests onto their neighbors. For example, a battered wife may not admit to a stranger that she has a need to learn how to respond to violence in the home. But she may indicate that she thinks her neighbors have such a need.

It may not be possible to tabulate the data gathered on community interest in specific programs. In other words, if only 20 or 30 interviews are conducted, you may end up with a *range* of 12 to 15 different services for which there is a recognized need, but no particular service which is identified more often than other services. It is possible, of course, that a majority of people will identify the same 2 or 3 family needs. But the interviews will probably only narrow down the choices for the family ministry committee to 6 or 8 needs. In that case, other factors can help committee members narrow down their choice of which needs to begin meeting first. The committee may talk to key community leaders (such as school principals, social workers or health professionals) to get advice on how to narrow the choices. Perhaps other churches or agencies are already providing certain services. The church may possibly feel more able (having more qualified people in one service area) to begin one type of ministry over another.

A general knowledge of the community will reveal other needs. Is teenage pregnancy a problem? Are drugs in widespread use in the schools? What about domestic violence and child abuse? All of these clearly point out family needs. Such information can help supplement the results obtained through neighbor-hood interviews.

Application Activities

1. If the results of the congregational questionnaire have been tabulated and are available to you, what is your reaction to them?

Do you find any of the data on the family pattern profile in your congregation surprising? Why?

How do you feel about the opinions of respondents on the strengths and weaknesses of their own families?

How do you feel about the opinions of respondents on the adequacy of the church's current family ministry and how it could most help families?

2. If the results of the neighborhood interviews are tabulated and available to you, what do you think are the clearest felt needs of community members who were interviewed?

Which of these do you think the church should seek to meet? Why?

What other information would you like to have before making such a decision? How would you use such information?

Planning for Family Ministry

Once you have identified family needs in the congregation and in the community, you will need to develop a strategy or plan to help meet those needs. This does not happen automatically. Knowing what needs you are trying to meet is important and valuable. But doing something about those needs requires careful planning, beginning with considering whether anything can be done at all!

After all, families will always have needs. Part of what holds families together and enriches family members is the constant striving to cope with the family's unmet needs. The family ministry committee must carefully plan programs in order to strengthen the family's ability to meet its own needs, rather than offer substitutes which may undermine the family.

Planning for family ministry is hard work. The ultimate aim is to provide services that are timely, relevant, and practical—so that the total well-being of families is enhanced. To do this requires constant attention to changing attitudes and needs, not to mention a creative resourcefulness that takes what is available (people, tools, buildings, knowledge, money) and applies it to the problem in just the right way. Above all, effective family ministry requires a system of planning that goes beyond management by crisis—putting out one fire after another—in the end being managed by our problems rather than the other way around.

One Approach to Planning

Planning for family ministry can be approached in many ways. Planning is deciding in advance what to do and why, how to do it, when to do it, and who should do it. Planning begins with a need, proposes a solution, then specifies the steps needed to implement the solution. In family ministry, as in many other forms of church ministry, there may be several possible solutions to the same problem, and many different ways to achieve any one of the solutions. The factors that make the situation in your church unique will help determine which is the best course for your family ministry program.

What is offered in *Ministering to Families* is one general approachto planning family ministry. The following steps are not a formula for success in family ministry. They are merely guideposts to help keep you on track, key elements of a multifaceted task. They follow a logical order, though many of the tasks must be performed simultaneously and often more than once.

1 *Define the problem.* Of course, the problem is that families in the church or community have a particular need. But *why* is it a problem? Often different people or family members define a problem differenly. The kids see nothing wrong with video games; Dad thinks they're a waste of money; Mom thinks they hinder the development of creativity. What exactly is the problem?

2 *State the objectives.* A need indicates things are not as they ought to be. Well, how should they be? How will we know when they're that way? If parents ought to be teaching their children about sex, what should the children learn, how, by what age, and with what results?

3 *Identify constraints to possible solutions.* Perhaps people don't have the resources to cope with certain family problems. Perhaps parents have no models to follow. Perhaps other pressures in society are too great. Perhaps people are complacent.

4 *List several possible solutions.* How can the various constraints be overcome and the objectives realized? If lack of child care for working mothers is the problem, identify all the places that could be used to run a dayschool. Who is available to run the program? How can they be trained? etc.

5 *Tentatively select the most feasible solution.* Choose one idea and consider it. Try to foresee any consequences of the proposed solution which might create other problems.

6 *Identify key people who should be involved in further planning* (before any action is taken). The fact that a planner has authority to make a decision does not mean that he or she has all the knowledge needed to make the best decision. Keeping communication channels open—especially among people who plan a family program, those who run it, and those who participate in the program—is vital to insure that program needs are assessed.

7 *List the steps or activities that the proposed solution might entail.* This is the heart of planning. What will be done? How? By whom?

8 *Set a schedule for such activities.* When will the activities take place? How will they fit into the calendar of other activities?

9 *Identify the resources which will be needed.* How much will they cost? Has the church budgeted for the expense? Are educational materials needed? Are meeting facilities required? Are the human resources (volunteers, coordinators, teachers) available? Do they have the needed skills to get the job done?

10 *Describe how and when the plan will be evaluated and modified.* Evaluation may occur at many different times—both before a plan is put into practice and after it has become a reality. What criteria will be used to judge a program's effectiveness? Who will do the evaluation? How will they do it? How will the results be used to improve, modify, or discontinue the program?

Planning for family ministry is a complex and neverending process. To keep from losing sight of the ultimate goal (serving families), keep two principles in mind: First, be realistic. Don't try to do too much at once. Consider carefully what difficulties may arise and how they will be handled. Do what is possible—be realistic.

Second, plan for success in the beginning. That may mean tackling a problem that is of manageable proportions, even if it is not the most pressing need the committee has identified. It is essential to have at least one visible success early in the history of a family ministry program so that people will support other family ministry programs in the future. If the committee's first attempts at family ministry are either failures or take a long time to gain support, the entire future of the family ministry is at risk.

Planning is a God-given tool for effective ministry. When Christian leaders pray for the Lord to lead them throughout the planning process, God will establish the works of our hands (Ps. 90:17).

Application Activities

1. Choose a family need identified through the congregational questionnaire, neighborhood interviews, or one which you feel is a pressing problem in your church. Describe how you would work through the 10-step planning process described above.

What is the need that you feel should be met?

1 Define the problem.

2 State objectives you would seek by removing the problem.

3 Identify any constraints which seem to hinder possible solutions.

4 List several alternate solutions.

5 Select (tentatively) one solution that seems most feasible.

6 Identify key people who should be involved in further planning before any action is taken.

7 List the steps or activities that the proposed solution might entail.

8 Set a schedule for such activities.

9 Identify the resources which will be needed.

10 Describe how and when the above plan will be evaluated and modified.

Presenting the Ministry

The timing and manner of presenting a new family ministry program to the church is important.The beginning of the ministry can set the tone for a long time to come; therefore, the time and effort put into planning the initial presentation is well invested.

Once the family ministry committee has started the needs assessment process, it can begin planning particular programs designed to benefit families of the church and community. If the family needs assessment was carefully thought out and well done, the family ministry committee should have a pretty clear idea of what types of ministries are most needed. The committee should then be able to identify one or more programs the church can offer, how they will be implemented, by whom and when.

Up to this point, the family ministry committee may not have received widespread attention in the church. Perhaps the elders set up the family life committee. The congregation may know the committee exists because of the congregational questionnaire—if the committee used this method of needs assessment. But the family ministry can no longer keep a low profile. When the committee is ready to implement its programs, it is time to go public. Widespread congregational support for and understanding of the family ministry is necessary for its long-term success.

An effective way to inform the congregation of the scope and intentions of the family life committee is to make a family ministry proposal for the congregation's suggestions, approval, support, and participation. Appendix D is an outline of a sample Family Ministry Proposal. Consider some important guidelines for presenting such a proposal to your congregation:

1 Make sure that periodic public announcements are made which mention that a committee is working on a plan for an exciting new family ministry program. These announcements will build anticipation. Also, many church people don't like sudden surprises, so this will condition them for the main presentation.

2 If people have already participated by completing questionnaires, the report to the church should reflect some of those results. Including this material in the presentation indicates that the congregation has had a vital part in the planning from the early stages.

3 Select an assembly time (preferably Sunday morning) where the initial formal proposal of the ministry will not be overshadowed by some other special event. People need to focus on this new approach.

4 In the presentation use people with high congregational credibility—the opinion-setters. Their endorsements are vital to other people's support.

5 In your presentation use visual aids (simple charts, lists, etc.) that are understandable and visible. Have something in print that gives more details about the ministry for members of the congregation to take home and discuss. You may want to distribute the handouts near the conclusion of your presentation, thus eliminating distractions.

6 Remember to simplify and condense the presentation. The committee may be far ahead of the general membership in their thinking. The presentation should be clearly understood by any person who has not had previous exposure to the idea.

7 Provide the congregation with names of people they can talk with about the new family ministry. Encourage them to give feedback to committee members. Invite them to be actively involved if they have particular interests or talents that are needed.

8 Media coverage should be used in announcing the new program—press releases, newspaper articles, interviews, etc.

Family Ministry Will Work!

The concept of ministering to families will work for three reasons: (1) it is biblical; (2) it meets a great need; and (3) it builds up and edifies the church. Your task as a church leader is to take these concepts and fashion them to the particular needs of your church and community. May God bless your efforts to build stronger families as you work together with others in leadership roles.

Application Activities

1. Read appendix D, a sample outline for a Family Ministry Proposal.

a. Can you think of additional points that should be included to ensure that the congregation will understand and support the family ministry in your church?

b. As you can see, the entire presentation builds toward point III, letter C, of the outline:

Congregational Response. What are some specific ways that the family life committee could plan (either during or after such a congregational meeting), to:

Get further suggestions from the congregation?

Get the congregation's approval of the family ministry concepts and proposed programs?

Get the congregation to participate in the proposed programs?

Group Activities

Preparation for Group Meeting

Instructions for All Participants

Check off the following items as you prepare for the group meeting:

- ☐ Read the chapter and complete the application activities.
- ☐ Look over the agenda for session 10.
- ☐ Make a note of any questions or comments you have about what you have read for this session (discuss them under agenda item 4).
- ☐ Write down your thoughts or reactions to the question given under agenda item 2, step A.
- ☐ Write down your thoughts or reactions to the discussion questions suggested under agenda item 4.
- ☐ Pray about concerns you've become aware of through your preparation for this session.

Leader's Instructions:

Preparation

- ☐ *Read the tips for session leaders (chapter 1).*
- ☐ *Read the chapter and the group activity agenda for session 10.*
- ☐ *Complete the exercises given in the chapter.*
- ☐ *Read all the leader's instructions (indicated in italics) before the meeting begins.*

Materials Needed

- ☐ *Newsprint, markers for all group members, masking tape, extra copies of the results of the congregational questionnaire and neighborhood interviews.*

Group Meeting Agenda

1. Opening

- ☐ *If this study session is part of the regular meeting of a committee or class, check with the person in charge on the procedure for introducing this part of the meeting. Otherwise begin this session with prayer.*

2. Large group activity (20–25 minutes)

This group activity uses what is called a "nominal group" process, since group members have a minimal amount of interaction with each other for the first part of the activity. The nominal group process has three steps, which are then followed by discussion.

A Each group member, working independently, writes on a sheet of newsprint three ideas in response to this question: "Based on the results of the congregational questionnaire and/or neighborhood interviews, what *long range goals* should we establish for family ministry both in our church and in our community?"

B After completing the above task, group members read silently what others have written. Then, using a different color marking and/or using the bottom half of the newsprint, everyone repeats step A. This time, however, the three responses should be numbered "1," "2," and "3" to indicate their priority. Group members are free to repeat what they wrote before or to use what someone else has written.

C After completing step B, the group members, again working silently, place a circle around the one item they feel is the highest priority for the church's family ministry. Members may circle any item, regardless of who wrote it or what it was numbered.

Discussion topics:

1 Discuss the question raised in step A above.
2 Do group members feel any tension between family ministry goals for the congregation and family ministry goals for the community?
3 Are the suggested goals balanced between educational/enrichment programs, outreach/service programs, and counseling programs?
4 Do group members feel a sense of closure on the question of long range goals, or is further discussion needed at a future time?

☐ *Tape twice as many sheets of newsprint to the wall as there are group members, including yourself. (Half of them can be used for agenda item 3, below.)*
☐ *Suggest that group members begin by drawing a horizontal line across the newsprint, dividing it in half. Ask them to write above the line in step A and below the line in step B.*
☐ *You should be the only one to speak from the beginning of step A to the completion of step C.*
☐ *In step B, members may write on the bottom half of any sheet of newsprint—it doesn't have to be the same one they wrote on before.*

3. Large group activity (20–25 minutes)

This group activity uses the same nominal group process as was just used, but focuses on *medium range goals.*

Repeat steps A, B, and C as above, but substitute the following question for the question raised in step A above: "Where should we begin? With what specific program or need should our family ministry begin?"

Discussion topics:

1 Discuss the question above. Why did members write what they did? If group members cannot reach a consensus, can they narrow their choices down to two (or three) ideas?
2 Are the programs realistic?
3 Are the programs sure to succeed?
4 Is further discussion about which programs to begin with needed at a future time?

☐ *If for some reason group members did not find the nominal group process in agenda item 2 enjoyable, or if time is limited, you may skip the nominal group process under agenda item 3. Simply begin with discussion question (1) above.*
☐ *Remove the sheets of newsprint which were used for agenda item 2 above, leaving one blank sheet for each group member. A chalkboard may be used instead, if adequate space for all is available.*
☐ *Additional leaders instructions for conducting the nominal group process are as given above under agenda item 2.*

4. Large group discussion (15–20 minutes)

- ☐ *Ask the group which topics listed below they would like to discuss.*
- ☐ *In addition, at this time individuals may bring up questions or comments they had about the chapter for consideration by the entire group.*

The discussion focuses on *short-range goals.*

Discussion topics:

1 Do we need to continue working on our long-range goals? Which members of the committee can do this (if not all), when will they do it, and how?

2 Do we need to consider further our medium-range goals? Is it possible to begin working on two or more separate programs? How will we set priorities for which programs to start first? Which members of the committee will be responsible for which programs? When will we meet again to plan this further?

3 Is it too soon to begin planning to bring a proposal for family ministry before the congregation? Can we set a target date for such a meeting? Who will begin working on the family ministry proposal?

5. Closing and prayer

Congratulations on the completion of this study course and the beginning of your ministry to families! No doubt you've done a lot of thinking and talking about your church's ministry to families. We encourage you to continue the plans you've made for ministry. The books listed in appendix E will add greatly to your knowledge and experience. Keep on growing!

- ☐ *Summarize the accomplishments of the group and close the meeting with a time of celebration and prayer and for the new opportunities for your church.*

NOTES

Appendix A
Family Ministry Questionnaire

Directions:
If you are 18 or over, please complete each item that applies to you. Your answers will be strictly anonymous so you can be completely honest. If you need extra space to answer any question, use the other side of the page.

1. Do any of the following family members live less than 25 miles from you? (check all that apply)

   1 _____ parent(s)

   2 _____ spouse's parent(s)

   3 _____ brothers/sisters

   4 _____ spouse's brothers/sisters

   5 _____ adult children

2. Does any relative other than your parents, spouse or children live in your home? (check one)

   1 _____ yes

   2 _____ no

3. Do you have step-parents?

   1 _____ yes

   2 _____ no

4. Do you think you have a strong family?

   1 _____ yes

   What do you think are the reasons it is strong?

   ____

   ____

   2 _____ no

   What do you think are the reasons it is not strong? __________

   ____

5. What area in your family life do you think needs the greatest improvement? (please describe)

   ____

   ____

   ____

6. How do you think this church can best assist you to increase

the quality of your family life? (please describe) ____________

____

____

7. What is your current marital status? (check one)

1 _____ never married (skip to number 13)

2 _____ married

3 _____ separated

4 _____ divorced, not remarried (skip to number 10)

5 _____ widowed (skip to number 10)

8. How many years have you been married to your present spouse? (check one)

1 _____ 5 or less

2 _____ 6–13

3 _____ 14–22

4 _____ 23–30

5 _____ over 30

9. Is your spouse filling out a questionnaire? (check one)

1 _____ yes

2 _____ no

10. Have you been married more than once? (check one) (If you are widowed or divorced, and not remarried, skip to number 13)

1 _____ yes

2 _____ no

11. How would you rate your overall satisfaction with your marriage? (check one)

1 _____ very satisfied

2 _____ somewhat satisfied

3 _____ somewhat dissatisfied

4 _____ very dissatisfied

12. What do you think has contributed most to making your marriage what it is (either satisfying or dissatisfying? _____

____

____

13. Are you a parent? (check one)

1 _____ yes

2 _____ no (if no, skip to number 17)

14. Do you have any children living at home? (check one)

1 _____ yes

2 _____ no (if no, skip to number 17)

15. If you have children, how many are in the following age categories? (list all that apply)

1 _____ number of children age 5 or under

2 _____ number of children ages 6–11

3 _____ number of children ages 12–14

4 _____ number of children ages 15–18

5 _____ number of children 19 or over

16. About how often do you have a special "family time" together with some spiritual emphasis as well as other activities (for example, worship, Bible study, family projects and games, special activities, family prayer, etc.)? (check one)

1 _____ more than once a week

2 _____ about once a week

3 _____ once or twice a week

4 _____ about 3 or 4 times a year

5 _____ rarely, if ever

17. Do you have any stepchildren? (check one)

1 _____ yes

2 _____ no

18. In your opinion, what is the attitude of this church toward single adults? (please describe)

____

____

____

19. Relationships with other family members are not always easy. The family life committee of your church wants to help enrich your family experiences through seminars, workshops, classes, study opportunities—whatever you need.

From the list below, please check concerns for which you would like us to provide help.

1 _____ parenting

2 _____ role of husband

3 _____ role of wife

4 _____ relating to in-laws

5 _____ relating to aging parents

6 _____ relating to adult children

7 _____ grandparenting

8 _____ divorce recovery

9 _____ finances/money management

10 _____ family worship

11 _____ leisure and recreation

12 _____ relating to teenagers

13 _____ interfaith marriage

14 _____ leading your child to Christ

15 _____ physical fitness for families

16 _____ accepting your own sexuality

17 _____ sex education

18 _____ alcoholism in the home

19 _____ drug abuse in the family

20 _____ child sexual abuse

21 _____ self-defense for women

22 _____ building self-esteem in the home

23 _____ television and video games

24 _____ premarital education

25 _____ marriage adjustment (newlyweds)

26 _____ empty nest adjustment

27 _____ household management for 2 career couples

28 _____ ministering as a family

29 _____ adjusting to death in the family

30 _____ estate planning

31 _____ coping with recurring illness in the family

32 _____ discipline of young children

33 _____ discipline of teenagers

34 _____ conflict resolution in the home

35 _____ establishing adult friendships

36 _____ teaching Christian values in the home

37 _____ what senior adults offer to the church

38 _____ parenting the handicapped

39 _____ parenting the gifted

40 _____ mid-life crisis

41 _____ family health through better nutrition

42 _____ adult single living

43 _____ other: ____________

____

____

20. In which of the above areas of family life do you consider yourself able to share with others meaningfully from your own experience? (write the numbers of the items below)

____

21. If a small group meeting, class, workshop or series of seminars were offered on the topics you checked in question number 19, would you and/or other members of your family be able to attend? (check all that apply)

1 _____ during Bible class

2 _____ on Saturday mornings

3 _____ on Saturday afternoons

4 _____ at a weekend retreat

5 _____ on Sunday evenings

6 _____ Monday evenings

7 _____ Tuesday evenings

8 _____ Wednesday evenings

9 _____ Thursday evenings

10 _____ Friday evenings

22. From time to time throughout the family life cycle, families sometimes require special support, encouragement, counseling or other services. For which of the following services do you or does someone in your family have a current need? (check all that apply)

1 _____ ministry to families of the handicapped

2 _____ coping with alcoholism in the home

3 _____ drug therapy/ rehabilitation

4 _____ dealing with violence in the home

5 _____ counseling/ministry to unwed mothers

6 _____ recovering from rape

7 _____ suicide hotline

8 _____ big brother/big sister program

9 _____ premarital counseling

10 _____ marriage and family counseling

11 _____ personal counseling

12 _____ vocational guidance

13 _____ providing food or clothing for needy families

14 _____ coping with unemployment

15 _____ refugee resettlement

16 _____ coping with the arrest or imprisonment of a family member

17 _____ coping with the disappearance of a family member

18 _____ relating to aging parents

19 _____ delivery of hot meals to the elderly or shut-ins

20 _____ providing meals for the family of newborns

21 _____ telephone check for senior adults living alone

22 _____ child day care

23 _____ babysitting

24 _____ neighborhood Bible classes for children

25 _____ ministry to the homebound or hospitalized

26 _____ combatting non-Christian influences in the community

27 _____ single adult issues

28 _____ reading for the sight impaired

29 _____ other: ____________

____

23. Ministry to families and family members in need (both in the church and in our community) is one way of serving the Lord Jesus Himself (Matt. 25:34–40). Which of the above services would you be willing to help *provide* for others? (On the line below, write the numbers corresponding to the items in question 22.)

____

24. What is your age? (check one)

1 _____ under 25

2 _____ 25–34

3 _____ 35–44

4 _____ 45–54

5 _____ 55–64

6 _____ 65 or over

25. What is your sex? (check one)

1 _____ male

2 _____ female

26. About how many years have you attended this church? (check one)

1 _____ 2 or less

2 _____ 3–5

3 _____ 6–10

4 _____ 11–20

5 _____ over 20

27. About how often do you attend church activities? (check one)

1 _____ 2 or more times a week

2 _____ once a week

3 _____ once or twice a month

4 _____ less than once a month

28. What is the highest level of education you have completed? (check one)

1 _____ less than 12 years

2 _____ high school graduate

3 _____ technical or business school

4 _____ some college

5 _____ college degree

6 _____ post-graduate work

7 _____ graduate degree

29. What is your primary occupation? (check the one that best fits you)

1 _____ homemaker

2 _____ self-employed

3 ______ skilled trade (carpenter, electrician, technician, foreman, etc.)

4 ______ semi-skilled worker (clerical, sales, delivery, etc.)

5 ______ professional/ management (teacher, doctor, lawyer, accountant, administrator, etc.)

6 ______ unemployed

30. About how many hours a week are you employed outside your home? (check one)

1 ______ 0–5

2 ______ 6–20

3 ______ 21–40

4 ______ 41–55

5 ______ over 55

Thank you for your cooperation. Your answers will give us an opportunity to meet your family needs in a better way.

Appendix B
Guide to Conducting a Neighborhood Interview

Considerations for family life committee:

____ *It may be wise to have two-person teams (preferably one woman and one man) conduct the interviews.*

____ *Members of the family life committee and any others who will be helping with the interviews should be given a chance to practice with each other before going out into the neighborhood. At this time, it might also be helpful to talk about the advisability of going beyond the stated purpose of the visit to sharing the elements of the Gospel message. Also, does the church have brochures about itself which could be left with those interested?*

____ *One way to adapt the interview guide to your local community is to add one or two items that ask about the effect of local events (such as school or factory closings, floods, etc.) on their family.*

____

Before the interview:

Address or place of interview:
____

____

Type of dwelling: __________

Date and time: __________

Introduction

Hi! My name is __________, and this is __________. We are from the family life committee of __________ Church. Our church is trying to plan programs that would be of interest to families in our community, and we're wondering if you would help us. Would you be willing to take about 10 minutes of your time and answer a few questions about possible programs our church could offer that might be of interest to your family?

1. No _____ (If no, thank respondent, record address above, and make sure no one else visits.)

2. Come back later _____

   (List date and time: __________)

3. Yes _____ (Proceed with interview)

Background questions

1. First of all, we'd like to know whether you are married and

whether you have any children.

Married: No _____
Yes _____

Children: No _____
Yes _____ Ages: _____

2. Do you have any relatives living with you?

No _____

Yes _____

If yes, who? ____________

3. Do you work outside the home?

_____ no

_____ yes

Approximately how many hours per week? _________

Service inventories

(Hand the person the Neighborhood Interview Inventories with *side one* facing them.)

4. I have a list here of programs or possible topics that are intended to enrich the quality of family life here in __________. Some of these might just be for adults, some might involve the whole family. Though these topics would be approached from a Christian/biblical perspective, we would offer them as a service to the community and would invite anyone to participate.

Which of these do you think would be of greatest interest either to yourself or to people in the neighborhood? You can just tell me the numbers next to the topics that you think people would be most interested in.

Write responses here: _____

____

(Have the person turn the page over.)

5. On the back are services that our church is considering providing to members of the community. Again, the people of our church would provide these services out of Christian love, and anyone in the community who needs them could receive these services. Which ones do you feel are most needed by people in the community?

(Record the item numbers here: _______________

____

Follow-up questions

(Retrieve the page listing the various services from them.)

6. Do you think of any other services that a church such as ours could provide that would be of value to people like yourself?

(Write down any responses; don't look to see if they are already mentioned on the inventory.)

____

____

____

7. Do you know of any other agencies that are already providing these or other valuable services to people in the community?

____

____

____

8. Can you think of any other way our church could be of assistance to you and your family?

____

____

____

9. Just one more question. Would you like one of us to get back to you by phone to let you know what decisions we actually make—or to inform you if we start offering a particular program?

no _____

yes _____

(If yes, make note of it and follow through with it.)

First name of person: __________

Phone: __________

Thank you very much for your help in answering these questions. Your answers have been helpful. Goodbye.

After the interview

Record the following:

1 Person's first name: __________

2 Was he/she head of household?

yes _____

no _____

3 Approximate age: __________

4 Your general impressions about the interview:

____

____

____

5 What, if any, literature from the church was left?

____

____

____

6 Would any additional follow up be appropriate?

no _____

yes _____ (If yes, what type?) ___

RETURN THIS INTERVIEW REPORT SHEET TO THE PERSON ON YOUR COMMITTEE WHO IS RESPONSIBLE FOR TABULATION.

Appendix C
Neighborhood Interview Inventories

(During the interview, this page is handed to the interviewee.)

Side One: Programs for Family Enrichment

Which of these do you think would be of greatest interest either to yourself or to people in your neighborhood?

1 _____ parenting

2 _____ role of husband

3 _____ role of wife

4 _____ relating to in-laws

5 _____ relating to aging parents

6 _____ relating to adult children

7 _____ grandparenting

8 _____ divorce recovery

9 _____ finances/money management

10 _____ family worship

11 _____ leisure and recreation

12 _____ relating to teenagers

13 _____ interfaith marriage

14 _____ leading your child to Christ

15 _____ physical fitness for families

16 _____ accepting your own sexuality

17 _____ sex education

18 _____ alcoholism in the home

19 _____ drug abuse in the family

20 _____ child sexual abuse

21 _____ self-defense for women

22 _____ building self-esteem in the home

23 _____ television and video games

24 _____ premarital education

25 _____ marriage adjustment (newlyweds)

26 _____ empty nest adjustment

27 _____ household management for 2 career couples

28 _____ ministering as a family

29 _____ adjusting to death in the family

30 _____ estate planning

31 _____ coping with recurring illness in the family

32 _____ discipline of young children

33 _____ discipline of teenagers

34 _____ conflict resolution in the home

35 _____ establishing adult friendships

36 _____ teaching Christian values in the home

37 _____ what senior adults offer to the church

38 _____ parenting the handicapped

39 _____ parenting the gifted

40 _____ mid-life crisis

41 _____ family health through better nutrition

42 _____ adult single living

43 _____ other: ____________________

____

____

Side Two: Services to Families in Need

Which of these services do you feel are most needed by people in our community?

1 _____ ministry to families of the handicapped

2 _____ coping with alcoholism in the home

3 _____ drug therapy/ rehabilitation

4 _____ dealing with violence in the home

5 _____ counseling/ministry to unwed mothers

6 _____ recovering from rape

7 _____ suicide hotline

8 _____ big brother/big sister program

9 _____ premarital counseling

10 _____ marriage and family counseling

11 _____ personal counseling

12 _____ vocational guidance

13 _____ providing food or clothing for needy families

14 _____ coping with unemployment

15 _____ refugee resettlement

16 _____ coping with the arrest or imprisonment of a family member

17 _____ coping with the disappearance of a family member

18 _____ relating to aging parents

19 _____ delivery of hot meals to the elderly or shut-ins

20 _____ providing meals for the family of newborns

21 _____ telephone check for senior adults living alone

22 _____ child day-care

23 _____ babysitting

24 _____ neighborhood Bible classes for children

25 _____ ministry to the homebound or hospitalized

26 _____ combatting non-Christian influences in the community

27 _____ single adult issues

28 _____ reading for the sight impaired

29 _____ other: ________________

____

THANK YOU FOR YOUR HELP.

Appendix D
Sample Family Ministry Proposal

I. **Basic Concepts for Family Life Ministry**
   A. Goals and Objectives of Family Ministry
   B. Biblical Basis for Establishing a Family Life Ministry
   C. The Need for a Family Life Ministry
      1. Results of the Needs Assessment Study
      2. Priorities for Ministry to Families in Our Church and Community
   D. Purpose of the Ministry and Methods of Accomplishment
   E. Method of Evaluating the Program
   F. Results We Can Expect
   G. The Distinctiveness of the Ministry

II. **The Functioning of the Ministry**
   A. Proposed Services
      1. Programs to Strengthen and Enrich Church Families
      2. Community-Oriented Programs that Emphasize Prevention Through Education
      3. Counseling Services
      4. Resource Center (Library)
   B. The Relationship of the Ministry to Already Existing Ministries
   C. Personnel Considerations
   D. Financial Considerations

III. **Where Do We Go From Here?**
   A. What Needs to Be Decided if the Concept Is Approved
   B. Timetable for Implementation
   C. Congregational Response
   D. Concluding Statement

Appendix E
Reading List for Family Ministry

The two most basic (that are useful) books in designing a family ministry for a congregation are the following:

Guernsey, Dennis B. *A new design for family ministry.* David C. Cook, 1982.

Guernsey is associate professor of Marriage and Family Ministries and director of the Institute for Marriage and Family Ministries, Fuller Theological Seminary. In this work he shows how the family is the most natural and effective place for the church to fulfill its mission. His approach is based on a life cycle model and utilizes a systemic understand of family relationships.

Sell, Charles M. *Family ministry: The enrichment of family life through the church.* Zondervan, 1981.

Sell is a professor at Trinity Evangelical Divinity School in Deerfield, Illinois, where he serves as the Director of the School of Christian Education. The book is an excellent blend of social, Biblical and educational dimensions that relate to the modern family. He emphasizes Christian education *in* the home (family nurture) and shows how it is best advanced by Christian education *of* the home (family life education). In order for the church to carry out its mission to the family, the church itself must become like a family. Practical application of these concepts and an extensive reading list make this work invaluable in developing a concept of family ministry.

Other important works that will supplement your formation of a ministry to families are as follows:

Anderson, Ray S. & Guernsey, Dennis B. *On being family: A social theology of the family.* Eerdmans, 1985.

Collins, Gary. *Facing the future: The church and family together.* Word, 1976.

Curran, Dolores. *Stress and the healthy family.* Winston Press, 1985.

Curran, Dolores. *Traits of a healthy family.* Winston Press, 1983.

Friedman, Edwin H. *Generation to generation: Family process in church and synagogue.* Guilford Press, 1985.

Gray, R. M., & Moberg, D. O. *The church and the older person.* Eerdmans, 1977.

Hinkle, J. W., & Cook, M. H. *How to minister to families in your church.* Broadman Press, 1978.

Howell, John C. *Church and family growing together.* Broadman Press, 1984.

Johnson, Douglas W. *Ministry with young couples.* Abingdon Press, 1985.

Louthan, S., & Martin, G. *Family ministries in your church.* Regal Books, 1977.

Mace, David, & Mace, Vera. *Marriage enrichment in the church.* Broadman Press, 1977.

Money, Royce. *Building stronger families: Family enrichment in the home church and community.* Victor Books, 1984.

Richards, Lawrence O. Developing family life ministries. In G. Peterson (Ed.), *Family life education.* Scripture Press Ministries, 1978.

Richards, Lawrence O. *A theology of Christian education.* Zondervan, 1975.

Richerson, Wayne. *How to help the Christian home.* Regal Books, 1978.

Sell, Charles. *Transitions: Stages of adult life.* Moody, 1985.

Sheck, G. William. *The word on families: A biblical guide to family wellbeing.* Abingdon Press, 1985.

Smith, L. *Family ministry: An educational resource for the local church.* Discipleship Resources, 1975.

Stinnett, Nick, & DeFrain, John. *Secrets of strong families.* Little, Brown and Co., 1985.

Wilson, Marlene. *How to mobilize church volunteers.* Augsburg Publishing House, 1983.

Wright, H. Norman. *Marriage and family enrichment resource manual.* Christian Marriage Enrichment, 1979.